Building Dashboards with Microsoft Dynamics GP 2013 and Excel 2013

Easily build powerful dashboards with Microsoft Dynamics GP 2013 and Excel 2013

Mark Polino

PUBLISHING

BIRMINGHAM - MUMBAI

Building Dashboards with Microsoft Dynamics GP 2013 and Excel 2013

First published: March 2013

Production Reference: 1180313

Published by Packt Publishing Ltd.
Livery Place
35 Livery Street
Birmingham B3 2PB, UK.

ISBN 978-1-84968-906-9

www.packtpub.com

Cover Image by Abhishek Pandey (abhishek.pandey1210@gmail.com)

Credits

Author
Mark Polino

Reviewers
David Duncan

Jivtesh Singh

Acquisition Editor
Martin Bell

Lead Technical Editor
Mayur Hule

Technical Editors
Kaustubh S. Mayekar

Dominic Pereira

Project Coordinator
Esha Thakker

Proofreader
Jonathan Todd

Indexer
Monica Ajmera Mehta

Production Coordinators
Pooja Chiplunkar

Manu Joseph

Cover Work
Pooja Chiplunkar

About the Author

Mark Polino is a Microsoft MVP for Dynamics GP, a Certified Public Accountant, and a Microsoft Certified Information Technology Professional. He is the author of the premier Dynamics GP related blog at `DynamicAccounting.net` and the creator and presenter of the successful presentation series *50 Tips in 50 Minutes for Microsoft Dynamics GP*. Mark has worked with Dynamics GP and its predecessor, Great Plains, for more than a dozen years.

He is also the author of the best-selling *Microsoft Dynamics GP 2010 Cookbook*, and the spin off Lite edition, both from Packt Publishing.

To my wife Dara and my children Micah and Angelina, thank you again for letting me take on another crazy project.

I want to offer a huge thank-you to Andy Vabulas, Dwight Specht, and Clinton Weldon of I.B.I.S., Inc. for their support. This book would not have been possible without their commitment to Dynamics GP.

To David Duncan and Jivtesh Singh who were kind enough to serve as reviewers for this book, thank you again for all of your support and suggestions. This is a much better book because of you.

About the Reviewers

David Duncan is a senior consultant with I.B.I.S., Inc., a Microsoft Gold Certified Partner based in Peachtree Corners, GA. David, who holds several certifications for Microsoft Dynamics GP and SQL Server, is also the co-author of another Packt Publishing title, *Microsoft Dynamics GP 2010 Reporting*. In addition to experience with implementing Dynamics GP, he has extensive experience in designing and providing business intelligence and reporting tools for clients who use Dynamics GP and Microsoft SQL Server. David has also served as a content provider for the GP portion of the Sure Step 2010 Methodology.

He has developed custom SSAS cubes for several GP modules such as Project Accounting and Fixed Assets that seamlessly integrate with Microsoft's Analysis Cubes for Excel product. David's combined experience with Dynamics GP and Microsoft SQL Server has enabled him to assist numerous clients in analyzing their strategic business plans by designing business intelligence solutions that allow them to incorporate data from multiple applications into a single reporting environment.

David, who holds a degree from Clemson University, resides in Rocky Mount, N.C. with his wife, Mary Kathleen.

Jivtesh Singh is a Microsoft Dynamics GP MVP, and a Microsoft Dynamics Certified Technology Specialist for Dynamics GP. Through his blog, which is widely read in the Dynamics GP community, he covers Dynamics GP tips and tricks and news.

He is a Dynamics GP Consultant and Systems Implementer and has been associated with the Microsoft Technologies since the launch of Microsoft .NET framework. Jivtesh has over 10 years of experience in development and maintenance of enterprise software using coding best practices, refactoring and usage of design patterns, and Test Driven Development. Jivtesh recently built a Kinect interface to control the Microsoft Dynamics GP 2010 R2 Business Analyzer with gestures. Later, he built a part of the GP Future demo for Convergence GP Keynote.

Jivtesh has set up a custom search engine directory for Dynamics GP Blog at www. gpwindow.com to help with easier access of Dynamics GP resources for the GP Community. With MVP Mark Polino he has also set up a Dynamics GP product directory at www.dynamicsgpproducts.com. Here are his blogs and website:

- Jivtesh's blog on Dynamics GP: www.jivtesh.com
- Jivtesh's custom search engine for GP blogs: www.gpwindow.com
- Dynamics GP products website: www.dynamicsgpproducts.com

www.PacktPub.com

Support files, eBooks, discount offers and more

You might want to visit `www.PacktPub.com` for support files and downloads related to your book.

Did you know that Packt offers eBook versions of every book published, with PDF and ePub files available? You can upgrade to the eBook version at `www.PacktPub.com` and as a print book customer, you are entitled to a discount on the eBook copy. Get in touch with us at `service@packtpub.com` for more details.

At `www.PacktPub.com`, you can also read a collection of free technical articles, sign up for a range of free newsletters and receive exclusive discounts and offers on Packt books and eBooks.

`http://PacktLib.PacktPub.com`

Do you need instant solutions to your IT questions? PacktLib is Packt's online digital book library. Here, you can access, read and search across Packt's entire library of books.

Why Subscribe?
- Fully searchable across every book published by Packt
- Copy and paste, print and bookmark content
- On demand and accessible via web browser

Free Access for Packt account holders

If you have an account with Packt at `www.PacktPub.com`, you can use this to access PacktLib today and view nine entirely free books. Simply use your login credentials for immediate access.

Instant Updates on New Packt Books

Get notified! Find out when new books are published by following `@PacktEnterprise` on Twitter, or the *Packt Enterprise* Facebook page.

Table of Contents

Preface   **1**

Chapter 1: Getting Data from Dynamics GP 2013 to Excel 2013   **7**

   SmartList exports   **8**

   SmartList Export Solutions   **9**

      Getting ready   9

      Creating macros   10

      Creating an export solution   11

      Navigation List export   13

   Report writer   **15**

   Microsoft Query   **17**

   SQL Server Reporting Services   **24**

   Management Reporter   **26**

   SQL Server Management Studio   **28**

   Analysis Cubes   **30**

   Third-party solutions   **32**

   Licensing   **34**

   Summary   **34**

Chapter 2: The Ultimate GP to Excel Tool: Refreshable Excel Reports   **35**

   Security   **35**

      Network share security   36

      Database-level security   39

      Excel 2013 security   42

   Running Excel reports   **43**

      From Dynamics GP 2013   43

      From Excel 2013   45

      Manual versus auto refresh   46

Modifying Excel reports	**47**
Reformatting Excel data	47
Modifying source data	49
Office data connections	53
Excel Report Builder	**54**
Restrictions	57
Calculations	57
Options	58
Publish	59
Summary	**61**
Chapter 3: Pivot Tables: The Basic Building Blocks	**63**
Creating pivot tables from GP 2013 Excel report data	**64**
Getting data to Excel	64
Building a pivot table	65
Creating pivot tables from GP 2013 data connections	**67**
Building a revenue pivot table	68
Copying pivot tables	**71**
Building the income pivot table	**71**
Creating a cash pivot table	72
Creating connected pivot tables from inside Excel	**74**
Building the sales pivot table	74
Adding a receivables pivot table	77
Excel Report Builder pivot tables	**78**
Creating Power View reports	**81**
Summary	**84**
Chapter 4: Making Things Pretty with Formatting and Conditional Formatting	**85**
Recap	**86**
Preparation	**87**
Get Pivot Data	**87**
Revenue	88
Net Income	91
Formatting	92
Icon sets	**95**
Data bars	**99**
Color Scales	**104**
Adjusting Color Scales	105
The green/yellow/red limit	**107**

Some more formatting	**108**
Summary	**111**
Chapter 5: Charts: Eye Candy for Executives	**113**
Recap	**114**
Bar chart	**115**
Adding a line	117
Pie chart	**118**
Speedometer chart	**121**
Building a doughnut	122
Cutting the doughnut in half	123
Building a needle	124
Finishing it off with sprinkles	128
Bar chart with trend line	**129**
Selecting charts	**133**
Sparklines	**134**
Preparing for sparklines	134
Adding sparklines	134
Sparkline idiosyncrasies	137
Deleting sparklines	137
Changing sparkline data	137
Summary	**138**
Chapter 6: Adding Interactivity with Slicers and Timelines	**139**
Recap	**140**
Learning about slicers	**141**
Creating slicers	141
Connecting slicers	144
Slicer orientation	146
Slicer options	147
Timeline	**151**
Timeline options	155
Summary	**160**
Chapter 7: Drilling Back to Source Data in Dynamics GP 2013	**161**
Recap	**162**
Learning about hyperlinks	**162**
Using drill downs in GP 2013	**165**
Drill down background	165
Using drill downs	166
Fixing the journal entry drill down problem	170
Drill down link structure	171

Drill Down Builder	**177**
Complex drill downs	178
Drilling down with GP 2013 and Excel 2013 on Citrix or Terminal Server	178
Drilling down to GP 2013 on Citrix with Excel 2013 installed locally	178
Other complex drill down scenarios	179
Summary	**180**
Chapter 8: Bringing it All Together	**181**
Adding headers	**182**
Cleaning it up	**182**
Adding a logo	**189**
Creating backgrounds	**190**
The Fill Color feature	191
Inserting a picture	192
Inserting a background	193
Good design	**195**
Final cleanup	**200**
Refreshing the data	**202**
Sharing	**202**
The quick option – e-mail	203
Network sharing	203
Hosting via SkyDrive	203
Downloading via SkyDrive	204
Downloading via SharePoint	204
Hosting via SharePoint Excel Services	204
Summary	**204**
Chapter 9: Expanding Pivot Tables with PowerPivot	**205**
PowerPivot Basics	**207**
Bringing Dynamics GP 2013 information to PowerPivot	**207**
Copying and pasting	208
Linking to a spreadsheet	210
Connecting via SQL Server	215
Learning about relationships	**218**
Creating a pivot table	**219**
Understanding the Excel data model	222
Other source options	**225**
About Atom feeds	226
SQL Server Reporting Services (SSRS)	228
Generating an Atom feed from an SSRS report	228
SSRS native connections	229
Windows Azure Marketplace	229

More PowerPivot options	**232**
Millions of rows of data	232
DAX formulas	232
SharePoint	233
Resources	233
Summary	**234**
Chapter 10: Slightly Crazy Stuff	**235**
Using built-in ratios	**235**
Current Ratio	**238**
Microsoft Dashboard	**238**
Negative data bars	**239**
Quick Analysis	**240**
Summary	**242**
Index	**243**

Preface

Welcome to *Building Dashboards with Microsoft Dynamics GP 2013 and Excel 2013*. Executives today want information faster and in an easily digestible format. That's where a dashboard comes in. The idea is to present key information that's timely and easy to understand. In this book, using the power of Microsoft Excel 2013, we cover the process of building an easily refreshable dashboard with information from Microsoft Dynamics GP 2013.

Throughout the course of this book, we're going to build a dashboard that looks like the following screenshot:

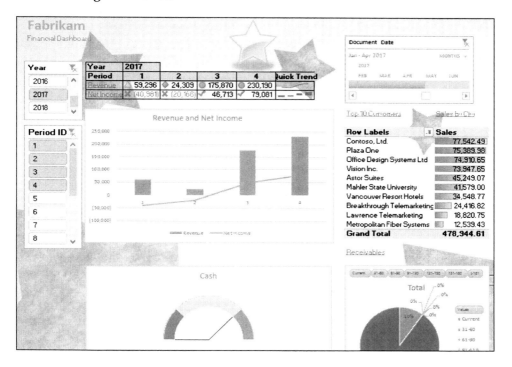

What this book covers

Chapter 1, Getting Data from Dynamics GP 2013 to Excel 2013, looks at nine major ways to get data out of Microsoft Dynamics GP and into Excel as a source for our dashboard.

Chapter 2, The Ultimate GP to Excel Tool: Refreshable Excel Reports, will walk us through the time spent with one of the best and simplest options for getting information from Dynamics GP into Excel 2013 the Excel reports included with GP 2013, after looking at all the other options.

Chapter 3, Pivot Tables: The Basic Building Blocks, will discuss the basic building blocks of any dashboard that are pivot tables. These tables summarize and group data in ways that make analysis easier. They are the core that the graphical elements rely on.

Chapter 4, Making Things Pretty with Formatting and Conditional Formatting, will explain Excel's conditional formatting that provides ways to add additional context to pivot tables and other elements by adjusting the way things look based on the information. Nothing spices up a pivot table like adding some conditional formatting.

Chapter 5, Charts: Eye Candy for Executives, will enable us to use a picture that is worth a thousand words. The right chart could be worth millions if it helps executives make the right decision. Charts provide the connections and revelations that are to present with just text.

Chapter 6, Adding Interactivity with Slicers and Timelines, will provide guidelines on a static dashboard that is just a fancy report. Users need the ability to interact with the information to discover new insights. Slicers and Timelines provide that controlled interaction.

Chapter 7, Drilling Back to Source Data in Dynamics GP 2013, will walk you through the great thing about dashboards that often provokes more questions. Questions that require details. Adding the ability to drill back to the detail behind the numbers adds tremendous credibility. It's even better when that drill-back takes you right to the transaction in Dynamics GP 2013.

Chapter 8, Bringing it All Together, will help us to finish up our dashboard, tie up all the loose ends, and really make it look good.

Chapter 9, Expanding Pivot Tables with PowerPivot, will explain us that just because our dashboard is done doesn't mean that we're finished. PowerPivot is an advanced Excel 2013 feature that takes pivot tables to places you can't imagine. You might not use them for your first dashboard, but you'll want them for your second one.

Chapter 10, Slightly Crazy Stuff, will acquaint us with the nature of this book, building a dashboard together, means that some things didn't quite fit for a specific dashboard but are useful for other scenarios. Those items get covered here.

What you need for this book

The following show the software prerequisites that are required:

- Microsoft Office 2013 Office Professional Plus is currently required for the PowerPivot functionality (blame Microsoft for the last-minute change)
- Microsoft SQL Server 2008R2 or 2012
- Microsoft Dynamics GP 2013 with the Fabrikam sample company deployed
- A web browser for links
- A willingness to think a little creatively
- Caffeine; if you really get into dashboard building, it can be a little obsessive

Who this book is for

This book is for the person that the CFO keeps asking about building a dashboard. It's for the controller, the analyst, or the senior accountant who knows that there is a treasure of information hiding in Dynamics GP, if they can just get at it. It's for the Excel power user who is tired of being held back by exporting data from GP and rebuilding information every month. If you're ready to start getting as much information out of Dynamics GP as you put in, this is the book for you.

Conventions

In this book, you will find a number of styles of text that distinguish between different kinds of information. Here are some examples of these styles and an explanation of their meaning.

Code words in text, database table names, folder names, filenames, file extensions, pathnames, dummy URLs, user input, and Twitter handles are shown as follows: "Save this file to your desktop as `PowerPivotSample.xlsx`."

A block of code is set as follows:

```
create procedure dbo.seeGLCurrentRatioKPI @UserDate datetime = NULL,
                                          @TimeUnit varchar(10) =
'Period'
as
    declare @CurrentRatio              numeric(19, 5),
            @PreviousCurrentRatio          numeric(19, 5),
            @LastYearCurrentRatio          numeric(19, 5),
            @CurrentBalanceAssets      numeric(19, 5),
            @PreviousBalanceAssets     numeric(19, 5),
```

New terms and **important words** are shown in bold. Words that you see on the screen, in menus or dialog boxes for example, appear in the text like this: "Select the first option on the top right, **Clustered Column – Line** and click **OK**."

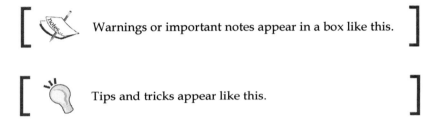

> Warnings or important notes appear in a box like this.

> Tips and tricks appear like this.

Reader feedback

Feedback from our readers is always welcome. Let us know what you think about this book—what you liked or may have disliked. Reader feedback is important for us to develop titles that you really get the most out of.

To send us general feedback, simply send an e-mail to feedback@packtpub.com, and mention the book title via the subject of your message.

If there is a topic that you have expertise in and you are interested in either writing or contributing to a book, see our author guide on www.packtpub.com/authors.

Customer support

Now that you are the proud owner of a Packt Publishing book, we have a number of things to help you to get the most from your purchase.

Downloading the support files

You can download the code support files for all Packt Publishing books you have purchased from your account at http://www.packtpub.com. You can also download the dashboard application along with the code bundle of this book. If you purchased this book elsewhere, you can visit http://www.packtpub.com/support and register to have the files e-mailed directly to you.

Errata

Although we have taken every care to ensure the accuracy of our content, mistakes do happen. If you find a mistake in one of our books—maybe a mistake in the text or the code—we would be grateful if you would report this to us. By doing so, you can save other readers from frustration and help us improve subsequent versions of this book. If you find any errata, please report them by visiting http://www.packtpub.com/submit-errata, selecting your book, clicking on the **errata submission form** link, and entering the details of your errata. Once your errata are verified, your submission will be accepted and the errata will be uploaded on our website, or added to any list of existing errata, under the Errata section of that title. Any existing errata can be viewed by selecting your title from http://www.packtpub.com/support.

Piracy

Piracy of copyright material on the Internet is an ongoing problem across all media. At Packt Publishing, we take the protection of our copyright and licenses very seriously. If you come across any illegal copies of our works, in any form, on the Internet, please provide us with the location address or website name immediately so that we can pursue a remedy.

Please contact us at copyright@packtpub.com with a link to the suspected pirated material.

We appreciate your help in protecting our authors and our ability to bring you valuable content.

Questions

You can contact us at questions@packtpub.com if you are having a problem with any aspect of the book, and we will do our best to address it.

1
Getting Data from Dynamics GP 2013 to Excel 2013

Microsoft Dynamics GP 2013 is a terrific enterprise reporting package. But when it comes to analyzing data, few tools can compare to the power of Microsoft Excel. When you put the two together and use Microsoft Excel to analyze the data collected in Dynamics GP, you can build something magical. By magical, I mean a dashboard that the CFO keeps asking about. Together, we will explore using the power of Excel 2013 and GP 2013 to build a straightforward dashboard.

We are going to build a great-looking, financial-oriented dashboard. Don't worry; we won't be doing any programming, and there are no Excel macros. This dashboard is built using nothing but native Excel functionality such as charts, pivot tables, and conditional formatting.

Before we can build a great Excel-based dashboard, using the data in Dynamics GP 2013, we have to get the data out of GP and into Excel. This chapter covers nine major ways to get data from Dynamics GP into Excel with a few extra options thrown in at the end. Some of these methods pull data from the interface in Dynamics GP; others bypass the interface and pull data directly from SQL Server. Generally dashboards are designed to pull from the database for the best performance, but sometimes you have to use what you have access to. In *Chapter 2, The Ultimate GP to Excel Tool: Refreshable Excel Reports*, we will start building the dashboard using my favorite way to get data out of Dynamics GP refreshable Excel reports.

By the end of this chapter you should be able to get data into Excel using:

- SmartList exports
- SmartList Export Solutions
- Navigation List Exports
- Report Writer
- Microsoft Query
- SQL Server Reporting Services
- Management Reporter
- SQL Server Management Studio
- Analysis Cubes

We will briefly look at some third-party options, and you'll also learn about licensing requirements around using Dynamics GP 2013 data with Microsoft Excel.

SmartList exports

Exporting from a **SmartList** to Excel is the easiest and most commonly used method in Dynamics GP to get data to Microsoft Excel. We'll practice with an Account Summary SmartList.

To export from a SmartList to Excel, follow these steps:

1. In Dynamics GP 2013, select **Microsoft Dynamics GP | SmartList**.
2. Click on the plus sign (**+**) next to **Financial** and select **Account Summary**.
3. Once the SmartList finishes loading, click the large, green **Excel** button to export this SmartList to Excel.

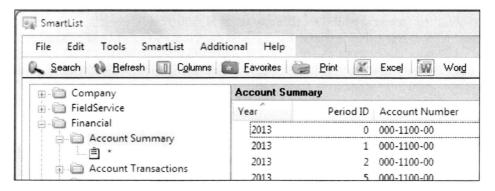

In 2010, Microsoft revealed a previously unreleased `Dex.ini` switch that can dramatically improve the time it takes to export SmartLists to Microsoft Excel. The `Dex.ini` file is a launch file used to control system behavior, and this switch changes the behavior of an Excel export. Instead of sending data to Excel one line at a time, the switch tells Dynamics GP to bundle the SmartList lines together and send them to Excel as a group.

This switch is unsupported and can render the results differently than the default export process. Please test this in your test system before using in production. The `Dex.ini` file is located in the `Data` folder of the Dynamics GP installation directory. To use this switch, add the following line to the `Dex.ini` file and restart Dynamics GP:

```
SmartlistEnhancedExcelExport=TRUE
```

SmartList Export Solutions

While SmartList exports are great for sending Dynamics GP data to Excel for analysis, they aren't an ideal solution for a dashboard. SmartList sends data to a new Excel file each time. It's a lot of work to export data and rebuild a dashboard every month. An improved option is to use a SmartList Export Solution.

SmartList Export Solutions let you export GP data to a saved Excel workbook. They also provide the option to run an Excel macro before and/or after the data populates in Excel. As an example, we will format the header automatically after exporting financial summary information.

Getting ready

We have a little setup work to do for this one first. Since these exports are typically repetitive, the setup is worth the effort. Here is how it's done:

1. Select the **Microsoft Dynamics GP** menu from the top and click on **SmartList**.

2. Select **Financial | Account Summary** on the left to generate a SmartList.

3. Click on the **Excel** button to send the SmartList to Excel.

4. Next, we need to turn on the **Developer Ribbon** in Excel:
    ◦ In Excel 2013, select **File | Options | Customize Ribbon**
    ◦ Check the box next to **Developer** on the right-hand side
    ◦ Click **OK**

Creating macros

A SmartList Export Solution allows you to run an Excel macro before or after the data arrives to format or manipulate the information so you only have to do it once. Let's record our Excel macro.

1. Click on the **Developer** tab and select **Record Macro**. Accept the default name of **Macro1** and click **OK**.

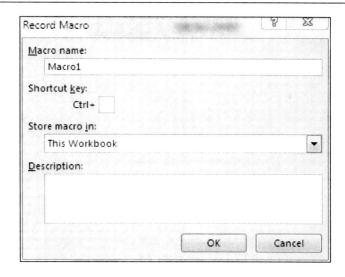

2. In Excel 2013, highlight Rows 1-5, right-click, and select **Insert**.

3. Bold the titles in cells A6-F6 by highlighting them and clicking the **B** icon on the **Home** ribbon.

4. In cell A1 enter `Sample Excel Solution`.

5. From the **Developer** tab, select **Stop Recording**.

6. Highlight and delete all the rows.

7. Save the blank file containing just the macro on the C: with the name as `AccountSummary.xlsm`.

Creating an export solution

Now that we've prepared our Excel 2013 workbook to receive a SmartList, we need to set up and run the SmartList Export Solution:

1. In Dynamics GP, select **Microsoft Dynamics GP** and then select **SmartList**.

2. Select **Financial | Account Summary** in the left pane to generate a SmartList.

3. Click on **Favorites**. Name the favorite Export Solution and click **Add | Add Favorite**. The favorite can be named anything. I'm using **Export Solution** for our example:

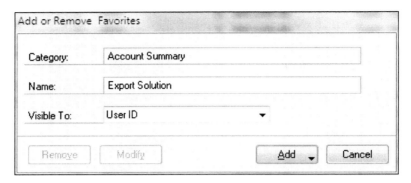

4. Back on the **SmartList** window, select **SmartList | Export Solutions**. Name the solution as Export Solution. Set the path to C:\AccountSummary.xlsm and the completion macro to Macro1.

> There is a length limit of eighty (80) characters for the document name and path. This can be a little on the short side, so it can be difficult to point an export solution to a file deep in a network file tree.

5. Check the box next to the SmartList favorite under **Account Summary** named **Export Solution**:

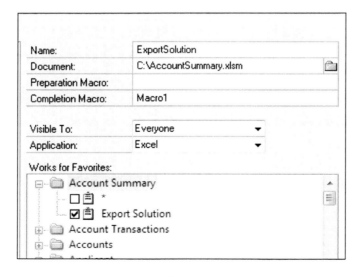

6. Click **Save** and close the window.

7. Back in the **SmartList** window, select the **Export Solution** favorite under **Account Summary** and click on the **Excel** button.

8. Instead of immediately opening Excel, there are now two options. The **Quick Export** option performs a typical Excel export. We want the second option. Click on the **Export Solutions** option. This will open the Excel file named AccountSummary.xlsm, export the data, and run the macro named Macro1, all with one click.

9. Click on the **Export Solution** option and watch the file open and the macro execute:

Navigation List export

Dynamics GP includes a feature called **Navigation Lists**. These lists provide centralized information views and access to tasks around common areas. For example, the Account Transactions List includes the ability to review journal entries, drill back to additional information, and enter transactions, all from a single screen.

Navigation Lists don't have a large **Excel** button like SmartLists, but they do include the ability to export to Excel.

To export a Navigation List to Excel:

1. Select **Financial** from the **Navigation Pane**.

2. At the top of the Navigation Pane, select **Accounts** to open up the **Accounts** list.

3. Check the white box in the header next to **Account Number** to select all the accounts.

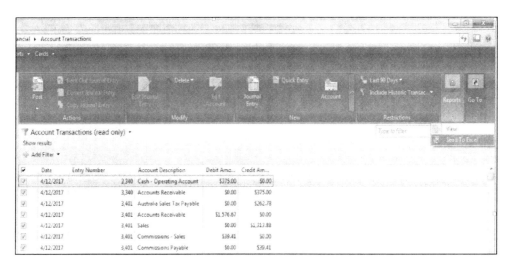

4. On the ribbon at the top, select **Go To | Send to Excel**.

 Like the Dex.ini switch that can improve exports to Excel from SmartLists, there is a similar, unsupported switch to speed Navigation List exports to Excel. To activate this switch, add the following line to the Dex.ini file and restart Dynamics GP 2013. The same caveats apply; test this on a test server first.

```
ListsFastExcelExport=TRUE
```

Report writer

The core reports in Microsoft Dynamics GP 2013 are still rendered using the included **Report Writer** application. More and more reports are available in formats that make it easy to bring them into Excel, but sometimes the information you need is most easily accessed via a Report Writer report. This is particularly true for reports that use temporary tables as part of the report generation process.

Report Writer can't export directly to Excel, but it can export to a comma-delimited file, a tab-delimited file, or a text file, any of which can be brought into Excel.

To demonstrate getting Report Writer data in Excel:

1. Select **Financial** from the **Navigation Pane**.
2. On the Financial Area Page, select **Trial Balance** under the **Reports** section.
3. Change the selection under **Reports** to **Summary**.
4. Select **demo** and click **Modify**.
5. In the **Year** section, select **Open**, set the year to **2017**, and click **Destination**.

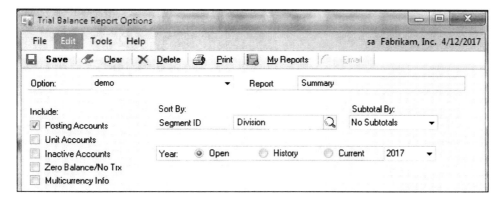

6. In the **Report Destination** window, uncheck **Printer** and **Screen** and check only **File**.

7. Click the file folder to set a location and filename and change **Save as type** to **Comma-delimited file**.

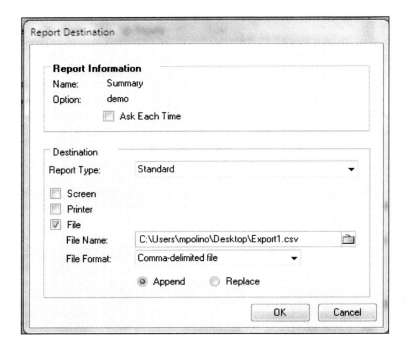

8. Click **Save** to close the window followed by **OK** and then **Print** to generate the file.

9. Navigate to the location where you saved the file and double-click the file name to open it in Excel.

For longer reports, you may need to sort the report to push page headers and footers together to make it easier to delete them.

On some reports, a single line of data won't fit on one printed line. In this case Dynamics GP wraps the line. This makes exporting these reports to Dynamics GP difficult. To prevent line-wrapping, add this setting to the Dex.ini file:

```
ExportOneLineBody=TRUE
```

This will force wrapped lines in the body of the report to export as a single line. This doesn't affect the headers or footers exported from Report Writer.

Microsoft Query

Microsoft Query is old technology. It's been in Microsoft Excel since at least Excel 97. It's still in Excel 2013 because it works. Microsoft Query is commonly abbreviated MS Query, and you'll see that used in this section as well.

In *Chapter 2, The Ultimate GP to Excel Tool: Refreshable Excel Reports,* we will look at deploying and using the refreshable Excel reports contained in Dynamics GP. For all of the power of those dynamic reports, one thing is missing—the ability to limit the data being returned from Dynamics GP based on parameters in the Excel worksheet. Excel reports allow filtering, but if a user only needs a subset of data, using filters is less efficient than simply bringing in just the required data.

Fortunately, there is another option. The MS Query tool included with Excel can work with **Open Database Connectivity (ODBC)** to connect to live data in Dynamics GP. What's nice about MS Query is that it:

- Is fast as Excel Reports
- Allows user-entered parameters
- Parameters can be entered in Excel cells
- Multiple parameters can be used
- Only the necessary data is returned, making them very efficient

This provides incredible control for live reporting of Dynamics GP data. However, there are no prebuilt reports that use ODBC connections, so users have to build these from scratch. Also, the user's Dynamics GP connection can't be used, so a separate SQL login is required for these reports. Microsoft was planning on adding parameter functionality to the refreshable Excel reports for GP 2013, but that feature didn't make the cut. That means that MS Query will continue to be useful into the future.

To demonstrate the power of Excel queries, we'll build a simple account summary report with a user-selectable parameter using Dynamics GP and Microsoft Excel 2013.

To build a direct connection between GP and Excel:

1. Open Microsoft Excel 2013 and select **Data | From Other Sources | From Microsoft Query**. This will start the MS Query Wizard.
2. Select the data source used to log in to Dynamics GP. The default data source is named **Dynamics GP**. Click **OK**.

3. If a user's network login is set up to access SQL Server, they can just click
    OK. Otherwise, enter sa as the username and sa as password. Either sa or
    another SQL user is required here. Encryption between the GP login and SQL
    Server prevents a regular Dynamics GP login from being used for this task.

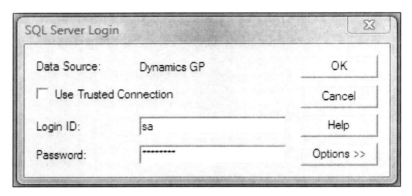

4. Click **Options** and select the **TWO** database. Click **OK** to start the
    MS Query Wizard.

5. We are going to use an SQL view, so click **Options** and check **Views**.
    Click **OK**:

6. In the Query Wizard, scroll to the view named **Account Summary**. Click on the plus sign (**+**) to expand the columns available.

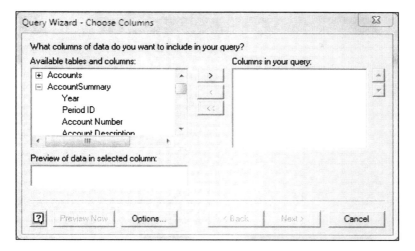

7. Find and select the column named **Year** and click on the right arrow (**>**) to add it to the **Columns in your query** box.

8. Repeat this process for these columns:

    °   **Period ID**
    °   **Account Number**
    °   **Account Description**
    °   **Credit Amount**
    °   **Debit Amount**
    °   **Period Balance**

9. The vertical arrow keys on the right can be used to reorder columns if necessary. Use these to move **Debit Amount** ahead of **Credit Amount**. Click **Next** when finished.

10. In the **Filter Data** window, select **Year**. In the **Only include rows where:** section, key 2017. Click **Next** to continue:

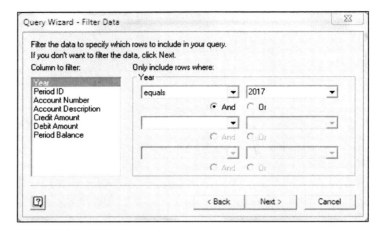

11. Click **Next** to move past the **Sort** screen and select **View data or edit query in Microsoft Query**. Click **Finish** to open MS Query and review the details:

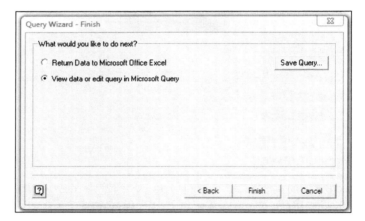

12. Once MS Query opens, select **2017** next to **Value**. Change it to [SumYear] and press *Tab*.

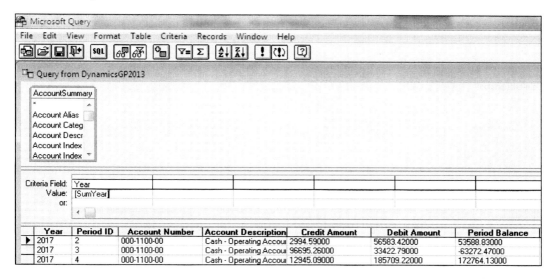

13. Enter 2017 in the box that opens and click **OK**. This step changes 2017 from a value to a variable. It then inserts 2017 as the initial value for that variable.

14. Select **File | Return data to Microsoft Office Excel**.

Experienced database administrators will quickly realize that they can use more complex SQL joins, views, and just about anything that they can come up with by using the SQL button in MS Query. There are some limitations though. Excel may refuse to allow parameters if the SQL query is too complex. The best option in that case is to wrap a complex query into a view to simplify it for Microsoft Query.

15. In the **Import Data** box, check **Existing worksheet** and enter =A5, then click **OK**.

16. The data from Dynamics GP will now show up in Excel:

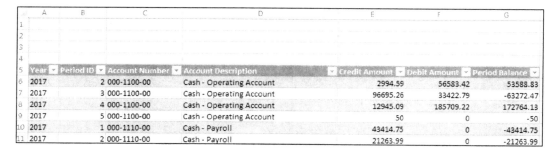

	Year	Period ID	Account Number	Account Description	Credit Amount	Debit Amount	Period Balance
6	2017	2	000-1100-00	Cash - Operating Account	2994.59	56583.42	53588.83
7	2017	3	000-1100-00	Cash - Operating Account	96695.26	33422.79	-63272.47
8	2017	4	000-1100-00	Cash - Operating Account	12945.09	185709.22	172764.13
9	2017	5	000-1100-00	Cash - Operating Account	50	0	-50
10	2017	1	000-1110-00	Cash - Payroll	43414.75	0	-43414.75
11	2017	2	000-1110-00	Cash - Payroll	21263.99	0	-21263.99

17. Now we are ready to add the parameters. In cell A1 type `Year`.

18. In cell A2 type `2017`.

19. Click on the **Year** heading from the imported data. Select **Data | Connections | Properties | Definition | Parameters**.

20. Click **Export Connection File** and save the file to create a portable Office Data Connection file with the embedded parameter.

21. Select **SumYear**. Select **Get the value from the following cell**. Key in =A2. Mark the **Refresh automatically when cell value changes** checkbox. Click **OK** and close all the other open windows:

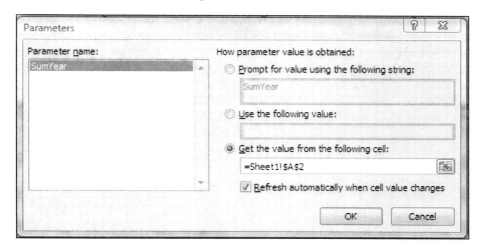

22. Change the cell value in cell A2 to 2016. Press *Tab* and all the values in the sheet will change to reflect data from 2016:

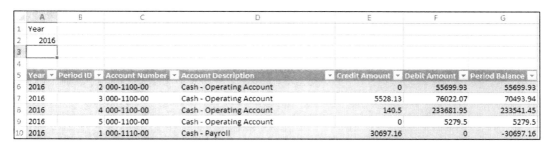

	A	B	C	D	E	F	G
1	Year						
2	2016						
3							
4							
5	Year	Period ID	Account Number	Account Description	Credit Amount	Debit Amount	Period Balance
6	2016	2	000-1100-00	Cash - Operating Account	0	55699.93	55699.93
7	2016	3	000-1100-00	Cash - Operating Account	5528.13	76022.07	70493.94
8	2016	4	000-1100-00	Cash - Operating Account	140.5	233681.95	233541.45
9	2016	5	000-1100-00	Cash - Operating Account	0	5279.5	5279.5
10	2016	1	000-1110-00	Cash - Payroll	30697.16	0	-30697.16

23. Save the Excel file. Reopen the file and change the year back to 2017; press *Tab* and all the values will update to 2017.

The part that drives users crazy is figuring out what table holds the data they need. When the Dynamics GP 2013 refreshable Excel reports are deployed, they use prebuilt views such as the Account Summary view that we leveraged here. Using these views is a great place to start when building a dashboard.

The Dynamics GP community is full of suggestions and tools to assist with finding tables too. Some of the more common tools include:

- The resource descriptions in GP 2013 found via **Tools | Resource Descriptions**
- The Support Debugging Tool http://blogs.msdn.com/b/ developingfordynamicsgp/archive/2009/08/07/ support-debugging-tool.aspx (short Link: http:// bit.ly/MSGPSDT)
- The DynamicAccounting.net table resource at http:// msdynamicsgp.blogspot.com/2008/10/lots-of- dynamics-gp-table-resources.html (short Link: http://bit.ly/GPTBLREF)

SQL Server Reporting Services

Microsoft provides prebuilt **SQL Server Reporting Services (SSRS)** reports as part of Dynamics GP 2013. Deploying SSRS reports is included as an option during installation, but they can also be installed later. SSRS provides an easy path to send information to Microsoft Excel 2013.

To demonstrate this, start in Dynamics GP 2013:

1. Select **Financial** from the **Navigation Pane** on the left.
2. In the List Pane above, click on **Reporting Services Reports**.
3. In the center pane, scroll down and find **Trial Balance Summary**.
4. Double-click on **Trial Balance Summary** to open the report.

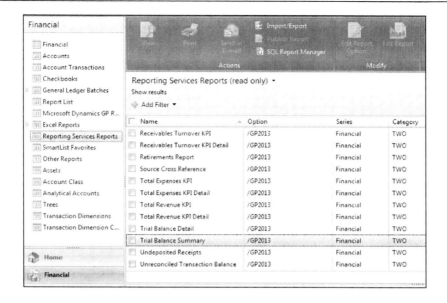

5. Once the report opens in a web browser, change the following criteria:

    ° **History Year**: No
    ° **Year**: 2014
    ° **Starting Account Number**: 000-100-00
    ° **Ending Account Number**: 999-999-99
    ° **Starting Date**: 12/31/2013
    ° **Ending Date**: 12/31/2014
    ° **Sort By**: Account

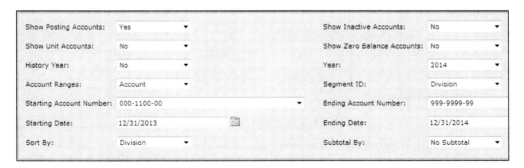

6. Click **View Report** in the upper-right to run the Trial Balance Summary.

7. Select the disk icon and click **Excel**:

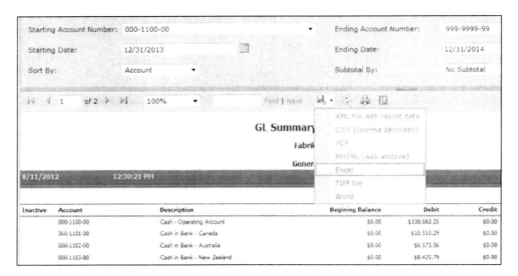

8. If a security bar opens at the bottom asking **Do you want to open or save...** select **Open**.

9. The Trial Balance Summary report now opens in Excel 2013.

Management Reporter

Management Reporter is a financial reporting solution designed to work with all of Microsoft's Dynamics products, including Dynamics GP 2013. As of now, Management Reporter 2012 is the current release.

Management Reporter reports are typically created as part of the implementation of Dynamics GP. The creation of Management Reporter reports is outside the scope of this book, but once they've been built, it's very easy to send these reports to Excel.

The process looks like this:

1. Open Management Reporter and run a report, displaying it on the screen.

2. Select **File | Export | Microsoft Excel (.xlsx)**:

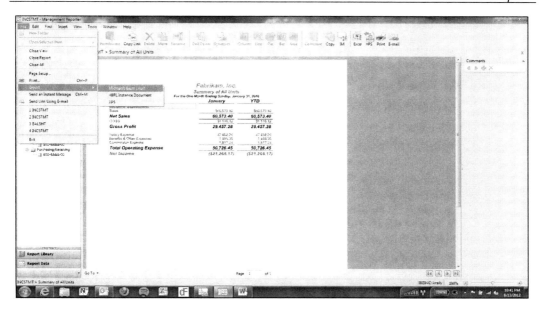

3. Select the elements to export to Excel and click **OK**:

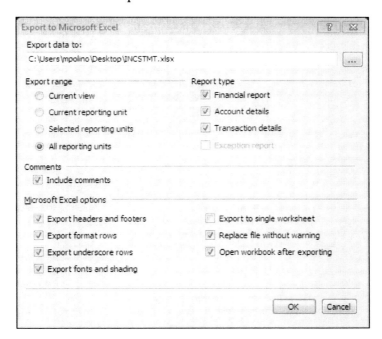

The export options are divided into a couple of major categories:

- **Export range** options control what level of financial information is sent to Microsoft Excel.

- **Report Type** controls the level of detail pushed to Excel.

- **Comments** controls whether or not comments are included in the export.

- The **Microsoft Excel options** section controls how the data is sent to Excel and include things such as including or excluding headers and footers.

When exporting to Excel, Management Reporter exports report headers and footers to the header and footer sections respectively in Excel. It does not send headers and footers to cells. In Excel 2013, selecting **Page Layout | Print Titles | Header/Footer** will let you access the exported headers.

Also, Management Reporter doesn't export formulas to Excel, only values. So the total fields that are exported to Excel will not update if you change any of the numbers in the Excel worksheet. This may change in the future, but for now, you can only export values.

SQL Server Management Studio

Microsoft Dynamics GP 2013 runs on SQL Server 2008 SP3 or later and SQL Server 2012. Some companies, in particular those with advanced users, allow read-only access to Microsoft SQL Server to make it easy for users to get just the data they want. Often this access is provided through the SQL Server Management Studio. Management Studio makes it easy to get data from GP 2013 to Microsoft Excel.

To see how easy this is:

1. Open SQL Server Management Studio.

2. Connect to the SQL Server instance with Dynamics GP 2013 installed using either Windows Authentication or SQL Server Authentication with a user ID and password. If you have access to SQL Server Management Studio, the login method and credentials will be provided by your database administrator. The user's GP login cannot be used.

3. Select **New Query**.

4. In the large, white box on the right type Use TWO and hit *Enter* to select the sample **TWO** database.

5. Type Select * from AccountSummary and click **Execute** to run the SQL query. The results will appear below the query:

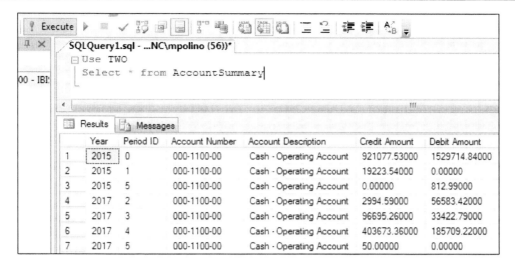

6. Choose **Edit | Select All** from the menu to highlight all of the results.

7. Choose **Edit | Copy with Headers**.

8. Open a blank Excel 2013 sheet. On the **Home** tab, click on the **Paste** icon in the upper-left to paste the data to Microsoft Excel:

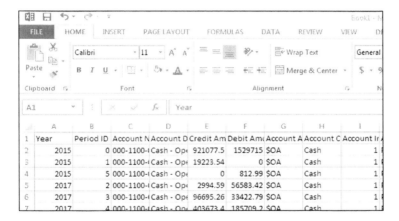

There is a setting in SQL server that will export headers when copying, even if you forget to pick **Copy with Headers**. The setting is found in **Tools | Options | Query Results | SQL Server | Results To Grid**. To activate it, check **Include column headers when copying or saving results.**

Analysis Cubes

Microsoft Dynamics GP Analysis Cubes for Excel is an **Online Analytical Processing (OLAP)** tool from Microsoft designed for Dynamics GP. Often the name is shortened to Analysis Cubes for Excel and abbreviated as **ACE**.

A full implementation of Analysis Cubes for Excel is beyond the scope of this book, but Analysis Cubes are one of the best sources of data for Excel-based dashboards, so we need to spend a few minutes with them.

Analysis Cubes for Excel takes data from Dynamics GP 2013 and places it in an SQL Server-based data warehouse for use with SQL Server Analysis Services. Usually this is done once a day due to the volume of data that is being pushed through. At its simplest, a data warehouse is a separate place to store information to report off of. Often the data is optimized to improve the reporting process as it moves into the data warehouse. A multidimensional or OLAP cube not only optimizes the structure of the data to improve reporting, it can pre-calculate and aggregate information to make reporting even more powerful.

The term "data warehouse" can be scary to folks. Some companies go through painfully long data warehouse implementations with careful definition of every element and arguments over how to normalize data for consistency. Forget all of that.

The beauty of a powerful ERP system, such as Microsoft Dynamics GP, is that the database design is known, documented, and doesn't change a lot from version to version. This means that a standard data warehouse can be built that works for companies using Dynamics GP and it won't require months of work to set up.

At I.B.I.S., we can typically install, set up, and train on Analysis Cubes for a company in about five days. That's it, a fully functioning data warehouse, plus training, in a work week. The Dynamics GP Analysis Cubes product contains well designed, aggregated tables for most Dynamics GP Modules. For people using third-party add-ons, a customized cube with appropriate measures and dimensions would be required.

After you work through this book and build a few dashboards, you'll start to bump into some of the limitations of reporting directly off of Dynamics GP data. These can include placing an undue load on the GP server, difficulty in finding and joining tables, and the struggle of calculating measures by hand. You'll also want to build more complex dashboards as you grow. Using Analysis Cubes for Excel is the next logical step.

Because ACE moves data into a data warehouse for reporting, data-heavy dashboards won't put a load on Dynamics GP. Also, because Analysis Cubes pre-populates and calculates information, complex calculations are available for reporting without having to create formulas in Excel. For example, in the next screenshot, you can see **Budget Variance**, **Current Ratio**, **Debit to Equity**, and **Gross Margin Percentage** are all available in Analysis Cubes to simply drag into a pivot table for use in a dashboard; no calculation needed.

Additionally, users have the option of reporting against the data-warehouse relational database or reporting against the cubes.

From a practical standpoint, using Analysis Cubes is very similar to the process we will walk through in *Chapter 2*, *The Ultimate GP to Excel Tool: Refreshable Excel Reports*, with refreshable Excel reports. The techniques used in this book to create a dashboard also work well when building an Analysis Cube-based dashboard. Analysis Cubes for Dynamics GP is included in the starter pack in GP 2013, so customers upgrading from previous versions have an even stronger reason to implement it.

For an in-depth look at some of these reporting solutions, including SSRS and Analysis Cubes, I recommend *Microsoft Dynamics GP 2010 Reporting* by Chris Liley and David Duncan from Packt Publishing.

Third-party solutions

All the solutions we have discussed so far are either included with Microsoft Dynamics GP 2013 or available as additional software from Microsoft. However, if you want to work with Microsoft Dynamics GP 2013 and Microsoft Excel, there are also a number of third-party solutions available. Selecting a third-party solution can be a challenging proposition.

It seems like every vendor remotely connected to reporting and Excel has put out what they term a **Business Intelligence** (**BI**) solution for Dynamics GP. Microsoft even referred to FRx, the financial reporting forerunner to Management Reporter, as a Business Intelligence solution. This may be technically true, but when you say "Business Intelligence", the average user thinks of a dashboard, not a financial reporting package.

The market has finally shaken out into a few categories with a lot of overlap. The options break down into reporting solutions that can produce dashboards, generally known as **Corporate Performance Management** (**CPM**) solutions, and more dashboard-focused solutions that can produce financial reports. For our purposes, I'm labeling all of these solutions as Business Intelligence. It's really about where the vendor places the emphasis.

Additionally, the choices break down into those that report directly off data in Dynamics GP, those that use a just a data warehouse, and those that use OLAP cubes for their underlying data sources.

The continuum for costs and sophistication generally break down the same way. Solutions that report directly off of GP data tend to be the least sophisticated and the cheapest. Solutions using a cube tend to be more expensive and more powerful. To help, I've pulled together a list of common, third-party reporting solutions. There are other CPM and BI solutions available for Dynamics GP 2013, but since this book is focused on Excel, I've only included solutions that are Excel-focused:

Excel-Based Corporate Performance Management options

Product	Direct reporting	Data warehouse	Analysis Cube (OLAP)
deFacto Performance Management – www.defacto.com	No	Yes	Yes
BI360 – www.solverusa.com	No	Yes	No
Vivid Reports – www.vividreports.com	No	Yes	No
Jet Reports – www.jetreports.com	No	Yes	No
Prophix – www.prophix.com	No	Yes	Yes
BizNet – www.biznetsoftware.com	Yes*	No	No
F9 – www.f9.com	Yes	No	No

*BizNet indicates on its website that it provides live reporting but it uses a cloud-based connection into Dynamics GP. It's unclear whether it uses a data warehouse in between.

Here are some BI options:

Excel-based Business Intelligence options

Product	Direct reporting	Data warehouse	Analysis Cube (OLAP)
BIO – www.bio4analytics.com	No	Yes	Yes
Qbica – www.kootio.com	No	Yes	Yes
OLAP Office – www.olapoffice.com	No	Yes	Yes

For the purposes of this book, we use the term "data warehouse". Some vendors use the term "data mart". Generally, a data mart is a specific subset of information in a data warehouse. For example, we might have a data warehouse of operational and financial information but we segregate just the vendor and AP information into a data mart for use by the purchasing group. Vendors seem to use them interchangeably with little regard for specific definitions, so for this book, we will use the term data warehouse for both.

The techniques shown in this book work pretty much the same whether you are reporting off a live connection to Dynamics GP, a data warehouse, or a multidimensional cube. Live reporting provides instant gratification. The use of a data warehouse improves the ability to scale reporting without increasing the load on the Dynamics GP server.

Licensing

Microsoft significantly changed the licensing model for Dynamics GP 2013. In Dynamics GP 2010, for example, accessing GP data via Microsoft Excel required paying for at least a "Light User" license. There was a lot of confusion in the community around what types of activities would require additional licenses to access Dynamics GP data from outside the application. Information from Microsoft was often confusing and contradictory. Users complained that they already had a license to access the data in their SQL server via their SQL **Client Access License (CAL)**.

While staunchly defending their "Light User" license, Microsoft did make a change for Dynamics GP 2013 and has significantly simplified the licensing. Accessing Dynamics GP data from applications such as Excel now only requires an SQL Server CAL.

Summary

In this chapter we've looked at a number of ways to get data from Dynamics GP 2013 into Microsoft Excel. Some organizations can be very restrictive when it comes to how accounting information is accessed. Having a lot of options makes it possible to still build an effective dashboard in spite of those restrictions.

In the next chapter, we will look at one of the best, and easiest, options for accessing Microsoft Dynamics GP 2013 data — the included refreshable Excel reports. In that chapter, we will start putting together the data that will eventually go into our dashboard.

2
The Ultimate GP to Excel Tool: Refreshable Excel Reports

The single best Dynamics GP 2013 feature for building an Excel-based dashboard is the refreshable Excel report. Excel reports are SmartList-styled reports that run in Microsoft Excel. They can be launched from within Dynamics GP or directly opened in Excel 2013. Even better, these reports represent live connections back into the Dynamics GP database. Refreshing the Excel report brings in the latest data from Dynamics GP 2013.

Refreshable Excel reports are easy to deploy, easy to update, and easy to work with. That's why they make a great foundation for an Excel 2013 dashboard. In this chapter you will learn how to:

- Deploy refreshable Excel reports
- Manage security to Excel reports
- Run Excel reports
- Modify Excel reports
- Build reports with Excel Builder

Security

By default, users can view Excel reports and data connections only if they have administrative credentials on the server that is running SQL Server and if they have access to the network share. Since this isn't a normal setup, users typically need reporting privileges in SQL Server before they can view the Microsoft Dynamics GP data that is displayed in data connections and Excel reports.

There are three areas of security around Excel reports deployed to a network share or local drive:

- Security to the network share/local folder
- Security at the database level
- Security around Excel

We'll spend a few minutes with each one.

Network share security

Realistically, network share security is normally going to be set by a network administrator. To shortcut this for administrators, the minimum required security on the shared folder is:

- **Change** for the share tab
- **Read** for the security tab

Now, for those of you who want the version that is longer than a Latvian wiener dog:

1. In Windows Explorer, right-click on the folder where you deployed the Excel reports and then click **Sharing and Security**.
2. On the **Sharing** tab, click **Advanced Sharing** and check **Share this folder**.
3. Click **Permissions**.
4. If the user or group already exists in this window, you can skip to the next step, otherwise:
    - Click **Add**
    - In the **Select Users, Computers, or Groups** window, enter the group or the users that you want to have access to the shared reports
    - Click **OK**
5. Select the user or group to apply permission to in the **Group or user names** area.

6. Select the **Allow** checkbox for the **Change** permission and then click **OK**.
    The **Change** permission is the minimum required permission.

7. Click on the **Security** tab.

8. In the **Group or user names** area, click **Add**.

9. If the user or group already exists in this window you can skip to the next
    step, otherwise:

    ○   In the **Select Users, Computers, or Groups** window, enter the group
        or the users that you want to have access to the shared reports

    ○   Click **OK**

10. In the **Group or user names** area, select each group or user, and then click the permission that you want the group or the user to have. The minimum required permission is **Read**.

11. Click **OK**.

 These instructions may vary slightly depending on the version of Windows Server used on the network or the user's version of Windows on a local drive.

By default, Dynamics GP 2013 deploys reports related to each company and each functional area in their own network folder. This makes it easy to apply different permission levels to sensitive areas such as payroll.

Database-level security

Access to information in the Dynamics GP 2013 database is handled a little differently. A set of fixed security roles is created automatically in SQL Server when Excel reports are deployed. All of these roles start with `rpt_`. These roles provide access to the underlying tables and views. The process to assign security is to add a user or group to SQL Server and give them access to the appropriate roles. The users that get added are not Dynamics GP users but either SQL Server users (different from the GP login IDs) or active directory users and groups.

This feels different from other aspects of Dynamics GP 2013 security in that setting security and assigning views to roles is all done from within SQL Server. The idea was to tie a SQL role to a role performed by a GP user, but in the end it feels a little clumsy.

To connect the SQL role with an Excel report to ensure that a user has appropriate access, you really need the spreadsheet from Microsoft that links the two together. You can find it at `https://mbs.microsoft.com/fileexchange/?fileID=e4bb6958-0f07-4451-b72c-f02784e484df`. (short link: `http://bit.ly/15C3XN2`)

In our example, we need access to the Account Summary Default Excel sheet. This sheet uses the Account Summary view. From the spreadsheet we see a number of roles that include the appropriate access.

84			rpt_project manager
85	**Financial**		
86	Accounts Defaults	Accounts	rpt_accounting manager
87			rpt_bookkeeper
88			rpt_certified accountant
89			rpt_materials manager
90			rpt_operations manager
91			rpt_order processor
92			rpt_production manager
93			rpt_warehouse manager
94	Account Summary Default	AccountSummary	rpt_accounting manager
95			rpt_bookkeeper
96			rpt_certified accountant
97			rpt_materials manager
98			rpt_operations manager
99			rpt_order processor
00			rpt_production manager
01			rpt_warehouse manager

For our example, we'll give a user access to the **rpt_accounting** manager role. In practice, it's not unusual to add all GP users to a single active directory group and give that group access to all the fixed reporting roles. This is particularly true for companies that don't use payroll and that don't have other sensitive reporting requirements.

To grant database permission using the built-in roles, we have to add the user or group to SQL Server and then assign the appropriate role(s).

To add a user to SQL Server, follow these steps:

1. Open SQL Server Management Studio and log in using either Windows Authentication or SQL Server authentication.
2. Expand **Security | Logins**.
3. Right-click on **Logins** and select **New Login**.
4. Click **Search**.
5. Enter the domain and user you want to add or enter the group that you want to add to SQL Server. For my example, I'm entering my domain and user name—**ibisinc\mpolino**. This could also be a group of users such as GPUSERS, for example.

6. Click on **Check Names** to validate the entry and twice click **OK** to finish.

The user has now been added to SQL Server. Our example used a domain user but you can also set up an SQL user. In general, a domain user is preferred because it eliminates the need for the user to manage multiple logins and passwords for reporting. Using a domain login also provides additional control to administrators. If an employee leaves, for example, removing them from the domain removes both their network access and their reporting access in one step.

To grant access to the reporting roles:

1. In the **Security | Logins** section, double-click the user or group that you just created.

2. Select **User Mapping** on the left.

3. In the upper-center section labeled **Users mapped to this login:**, check the box next to the company that you want to grant report access to. For our example, select **TWO**.

4. In the lower-center section named **Database role membership for: TWO**, check the box next to **rpt_Accounting Manager**:

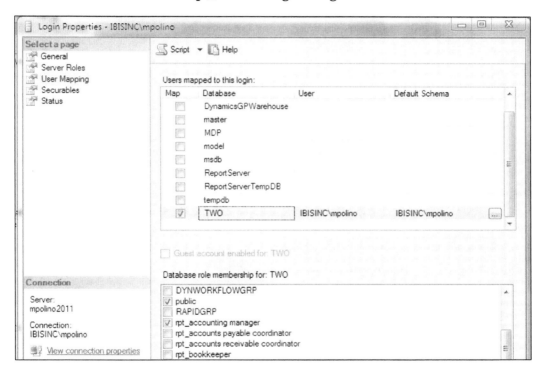

5. Click **OK** to continue.

The user now has rights to access the **TWO AccountSummary** default report that we've been working with and any other reports available as part of the **rpt_ Accounting** Manager role.

Excel 2013 security

As you connect with database connections in Excel, a security bar may pop up with the message **SECURITY WARNING External Data Connections have been disabled**:

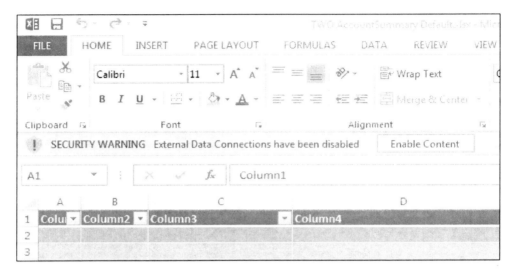

This is an Excel security feature designed to prevent malicious code from running without the user's knowledge. In our case, however, we deployed the reports, we are running them on our network, and controlling access. This is about as secure as it's going to get and the message is really annoying for users. Let's turn it off.

To disable the Excel security message for these files:

1. Open Microsoft Excel 2013 and select **File** | **Options** | **Trust Center**.
2. Select **Trusted Locations**.
3. Click **Add new location**.
4. Browse to the location where you deployed the Excel reports. In my example, I used c:\GP2013XL. Click **OK**.

5. Check the box marked **Subfolders of this location are also trusted** and click **OK**:

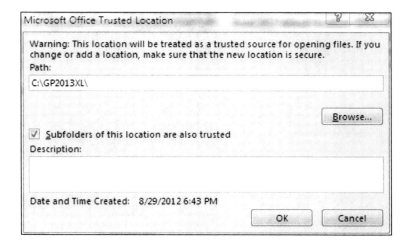

6. Click **OK** twice to exit.

Now, when you run the Excel reports in the next section, the reports will open in Excel 2013 without the security warning.

 Microsoft offers a great Knowledge Base article on Excel reports and security at `http://support.microsoft.com/kb/949524`.

Running Excel reports

Our next step is to run an Excel report. These reports can be run from Dynamics GP 2013 or they can be directly opened in Excel 2013. We will look at both of these options.

From Dynamics GP 2013

To run an Excel report from within Dynamics GP:

1. In the Navigation Pane on the left, click **Financial**. The List Pane above will change to show financial items.

2. In the List Pane, click **Excel Reports**.

3. In the Navigation List in the center, select **TWO AccountSummary Default**. Make sure that you select the **Option** column's options that includes **Reports**:

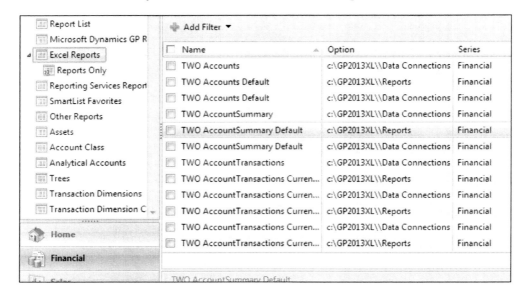

 Options that contain the word **Reports** open Excel reports. Options with **Data Connections** in the string indicate the data connector to build a new report, not an actual report. You can limit the Excel reports list to just **Reports** or **Data Connections** with the **Add Filter** button just above the Excel reports list.

4. Double-click on the **TWO AccountSummary Default** item.
5. We disabled the security warning earlier, but just in case, if Excel 2013 opens with a security warning at the top of the worksheet, click **Enable Content**. Then go back and review the section on Excel 2013 security earlier in this chapter.

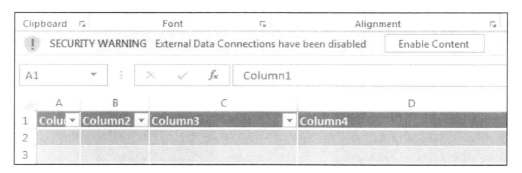

6. Excel will open with live data from Microsoft Dynamics GP:

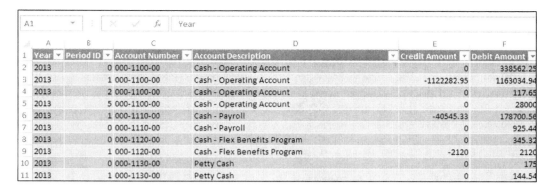

7. As a test, highlight rows seven through ten (**7-10**) on the left and press the *Delete* key.
8. Select **Data | Refresh All** on the ribbon. Excel 2013 will reconnect to Dynamics GP and bring back in the latest data.

From Excel 2013

To accomplish this same task from Excel 2013, follow these steps:

1. Open Windows Explorer and navigate to the location where you deployed the reports at the beginning of this chapter. In my example, the reports were deployed to C:\GP2013XL\.
2. Drill down through the folders to **Reports | TWO | Financial**. This represents the report storage for the sample company's (**TWO**) financial reports:

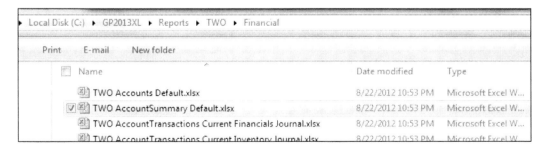

3. Double-click on **TWO AccountSummary Default.xlsx**.
4. Excel 2013 will open with live data from Dynamics GP.

Manual versus auto refresh

Excel reports are refreshable, but that doesn't mean that they have to refresh automatically.

Often accountants ask about saving a static version of the file. They love the idea of refreshing data, but they want it to happen on their terms. Most accountants prefer information that doesn't change once it's been finalized, so this request is perfectly natural. By default, the Dynamics GP 2013 connections are designed to refresh automatically when the file is opened, but you can control this.

To understand how to control the refresh options:

1. Start with the **TWO AccountSummary Default** Excel file that you already have open.

2. In Excel, select the **Data** tab followed by **Connections | Properties**:

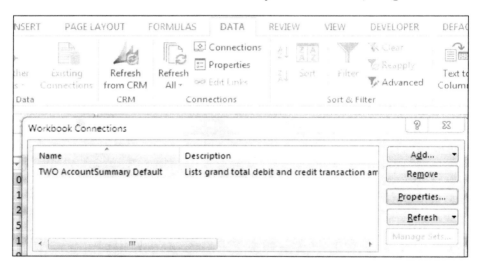

3. Uncheck the **Refresh data when opening the file** box and click **OK**.

4. Click **Close** to return to the worksheet in Excel.

5. To validate that this worked, select rows seven through ten (7-10) in the Excel sheet and press *Delete*.

6. Save the Excel sheet to your desktop as TWO AccountSummary Default Manual Refresh and close Excel 2013.

7. To reopen the file, double-click TWO AccountSummary Default Manual Refresh on the desktop.

8. Excel will open with data, and rows seven through ten (7-10) will be blank. The sheet did not refresh automatically.

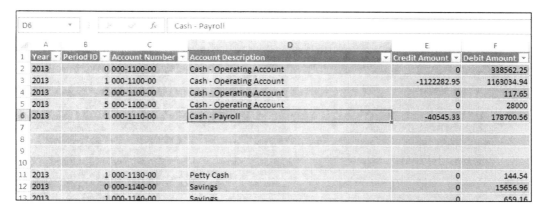

9. To manually refresh the sheet, right-click anywhere in the data area and click **Refresh** or select **Data | Refresh All**.

 If you save a report or connector with a different name into one of the network share or locally deployed Excel report folders, that report will appear as an Excel report in Dynamics GP as well.

Modifying Excel reports

Despite the power of refreshable Excel reports, there can be times where you can't get to the information you need. Maybe the information is there, but it isn't formatted in the way that you want. The beauty of Excel reports is that we have the power of Excel and SQL at our fingertips. In this section, we will look at some ways to reformat data in Excel and some options to get additional information into an Excel report.

Reformatting Excel data

It is common to want to reformat information after it arrives in Excel. For example, in the Account Summary worksheet that we've been working with, it can be helpful to combine Year and Period to make sorting and understanding data easier. Because Dynamics GP 2013 automatically puts Excel data into tables, this is easy to do using Excel formulas. Excel 2013 makes it even easier with its new **Flash Fill** feature. Let's look at how to do it both ways.

To combine Year and Period with a formula:

1. Open the **TWO AccountSummary Report**.

2. If Excel 2013 opens with a security warning at the top of the worksheet, click **Enable Content**.

3. In cell G1, type the header: YearMonth. Because the Excel report uses a table, this column turns blue indicating that it has been added to the end of the table.

4. In cell G2, type the formula: =A2&"-"&RIGHT("0"&B2,2). The first part of this formula takes the year value from cell A2 and adds a dash to separate year and month. The second part adds a zero to the month and takes the rightmost two characters. This unifies all months to two digits.

5. Press *Tab* to move to the next field. Because this is a table in Excel, the formula automatically fills down into all the rows in the table.

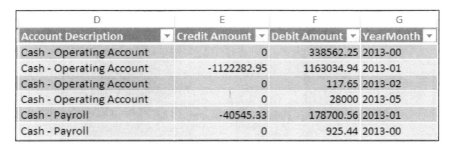

D Account Description	E Credit Amount	F Debit Amount	G YearMonth
Cash - Operating Account	0	338562.25	2013-00
Cash - Operating Account	-1122282.95	1163034.94	2013-01
Cash - Operating Account	0	117.65	2013-02
Cash - Operating Account	0	28000	2013-05
Cash - Payroll	-40545.33	178700.56	2013-01
Cash - Payroll	0	925.44	2013-00

While this is definitely easier than having to copy down the formula, this option was available in previous versions of Excel. Excel 2013 introduces a new Flash Fill feature that makes this even easier, no formulas required.

To accomplish the same thing with Flash Fill:

1. Close and reopen **TWO AccountSummary Report** without saving.

2. Select the header for column **C**, right-click, and select **Insert**.

3. In cell C1, type the header: YearMonth.

4. In cell C2, we need to show Excel what the final output should look like. You'll need to type the year and month information from cells A2 and B2 in the format that you want. Type 2013-00 and hit *Enter*.

5. Excel isn't quite sure what you want yet. Move to cell C3 and type the year and month from A3 and B3. Type `2013-01` and press *Enter*.

6. Repeat this one more time with information from cells A4 and B4 in cell C4. Type `2013-01` and press *Enter*.

This is a fairly complex pattern but, as you can see in the next screenshot, by the third try Excel has figured it out. Excel often figures out common patterns such as last name, first name on the first try. When you hit *Enter* on the third line, Excel copies the pattern all the way down to the end of the list, no formulas required.

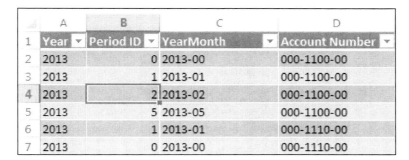

This is just a sample of the kinds of transformations that can be easily done with Excel 2013.

Flash Fill is new and it's not perfect. Flash Fill results aren't formulas, so they don't get automatically updated when the file is refreshed, but they are easy to build and I suspect that Microsoft will continue to add to this feature.

Modifying source data

Excel reports provide live data from Dynamics GP via a connection to Microsoft SQL Server. This connection can be modified to provide additional information not included by default. Like SmartLists, many of the Excel reports rely on views. Users familiar with SmartLists know that you can click on **Columns** | **Add** to see additional information available on a SmartList. Similarly, Excel reports don't always show all the columns that are available in the view. With that in mind, we'll look at how you can modify the source behind an Excel report.

To modify an Excel report:

1. Close and reopen **TWO AccountSummary Report** without saving.

2. Select **Data | Connections | Properties**. Click on the **Definition** tab:

3. Clear all the text from the **Command text** box.

4. In the **Command text** box, type `Select * from AccountSummary` and click **OK**:

5. If a warning dialog appears that begins with **The connection in this workbook will no longer be identical to the connection defined in the external file...**, click **Yes** to continue:

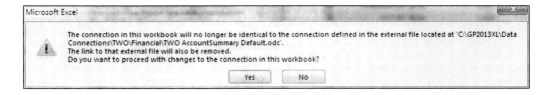

Connections and this message are covered in detail later in this chapter.

6. Select **Close** to close the window. Excel will populate with significantly more columns than before.

7. This is now saved as your new AccountSummary connection.

AK	AL	AM	AN
Segments ▾	Ledger Name ▾	Ledger Description ▾	Account Index For Drillback ▾
3	BASE	Base Ledger	dgpp://DynamicsGPDrillBack/?
3	BASE	Base Ledger	dgpp://DynamicsGPDrillBack/?
3	BASE	Base Ledger	dgpp://DynamicsGPDrillBack/?
3	BASE	Base Ledger	dgpp://DynamicsGPDrillBack/?
3	BASE	Base Ledger	dgpp://DynamicsGPDrillBack/?
3	BASE	Base Ledger	dgpp://DynamicsGPDrillBack/?
3	BASE	Base Ledger	dgpp://DynamicsGPDrillBack/?
3	BASE	Base Ledger	dgpp://DynamicsGPDrillBack/?
3	BASE	Base Ledger	dgpp://DynamicsGPDrillBack/?

In the original Account Summary worksheet that we've been working with, only columns **A** through **F** were populated. Now the sheet goes all the way out to column **AN**. We've gone from six columns of data to 40, just like that.

The **Command text** box is much more robust than the **SQL** box used in Microsoft Query. It's possible to create complex SQL commands in a tool such as SQL Server Management Studio and paste them into the **Command text** box. This means that even if you are not an SQL guru, if you can convince your company's Database Administrator (DBA) to write the SQL for you, all you have to do is paste it into Excel.

It's also possible for you, or your DBA, to simply wrap a complex query into an SQL view. This makes it very easy to use complex queries with Excel reports. That way, if the query needs to change, all that is required is a change to the underlying view. A user doesn't need to change every spreadsheet in the company.

 There are some great resources for more complex queries including my SQL resources at **DynamicAccounting.net** (http://bit.ly/ DynAcctSQL) and fellow Packt Publishing author Victoria Yudin's site (http://www.victoriayudin.com).

Office data connections

When you deploy Dynamics GP 2013's Excel reports, you also deploy a set of **Office Data Connection** (**ODC**) files. These files provide the connection details from Excel 2013 back into Dynamics GP data stored in SQL Server.

Connection information can be stored in the Excel file itself using the **Connection Properties** window via **Data | Connections | Properties | Definition**, or it can be stored in an ODC file. Connection information stored in the Excel file is only available to that file. Connections stored in an ODC file are available to share and re-use.

For example, if we build a great financial dashboard and a colleague wants to build a variation based off of the same data, we can give them our Excel file. They'll have to tear out our dashboard to get back to the core data and then start over, or we can point them to the ODC file that we've saved allowing them to report off the same subset of data.

In an earlier example, when we changed the SQL query, we got an error message stating: **The connection in this workbook will no longer be identical to the connection defined in the external file**. This message is warning us that this Excel file will no longer be using the ODC file in its connection. It's usually a good idea to save the revised connection as an ODC file to make it available later. Try not to overwrite the core GP ODC files. They are useful as a baseline, and while they can be easily redeployed, redeploying them will wipe out any changes to files with the same name.

To save connection information to an ODC file:

1. Select **Data | Connections | Properties | Definition** in Excel 2013.
2. After any changes have been made, click **Export Connection File**, provide a name and location, then click **Save**.

To apply a connection file to a specific workbook in place of a local connection:

1. Select **Data | Connections | Properties | Definition** in Excel 2013.
2. Click **Browse**. Browse to and select the appropriate ODC file and click **Open**.

3. Check the **Always use connection file** setting to force Excel to use the ODC file:

Excel Report Builder

For those who want to build their own Excel reports without learning even minimal SQL or messing with Excel's connection properties, Microsoft offers an optional **Excel Report Builder** module as a component of SmartList builder. Excel Report Builder allows users to build and deploy their own Excel reports. A full treatment of Excel Report Builder is beyond what we can cover in this chapter, but we'll hit the highlights, along with a few things that don't normally get covered. First we'll look at building a basic report with Excel Report Builder and then we'll explore some of the special things you can do with it.

To build a basic report with Excel Report Builder, open Dynamics GP 2013 and follow these steps:

1. In GP 2013, select **Microsoft Dynamics GP | Tools | SmartList Builder | Excel Report Builder | Excel Report Builder**.

2. In **Report ID**, type SUMMARY EXAMPLE to create a new report.

3. Leave **Report Type** set to **List**, but note that you can set this to **Pivot Table** and export this to Excel as a pivot table. We'll talk more about pivot tables in *Chapter 3*, *Pivot Tables: The Basic Building Blocks*.

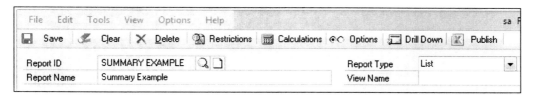

4. Click the plus symbol (**+**) next to **Tables** and pick **Microsoft Dynamics GP Table**.

5. Use the following settings and click **Save** when done:
    ° **Product: Microsoft Dynamics GP**
    ° **Series: Financial**
    ° **Table: Account Summary Master View**

6. Check **Display** next to the following items:
    ° **Year**
    ° **Period ID**
    ° **Account Index**

      ° **Credit Amount**

      ° **Debit Amount**

Field Name	Display Name	→	Display	
Account Index	Account Index		✓	
Year	Year		✓	
Period ID	Period ID		✓	
Ledger ID	Ledger ID		☐	
Account Number:Account_Segmen	Account Number:Account_Segment_Pool1		☐	
Account Number:Account_Segmen	Account Number:Account_Segment_Pool2		☐	
Account Number:Account_Segmen	Account Number:Account_Segment_Pool3		☐	
Account Number:Account_Segmen	Account Number:Account_Segment_Pool4		☐	
Account Number:Account_Segmen	Account Number:Account_Segment_Pool5		☐	
Account Category Number	Account Category Number		☐	
Period Balance	Period Balance		☐	
Credit Amount	Credit Amount		✓	
Debit Amount	Debit Amount		✓	
Account Alias	Account Alias		☐	
Main Account Segment	Main Account Segment		☐	

All Account Summary Master View Fields; by Field Position

7. I know, you're wondering where the account number is. To set the account number:

      ° Select **Account Index** and click the expansion button (blue arrow) next to **Display Name**.

      ° Check the **Account Index – Show Account Number** box. This swaps out the account index for the full account number.

> The expansion button (blue arrow) provides additional options for a line, depending on the type of data the line contains. For example, options can provide the ability to show the percentage symbol and negatives.

8. Click on the **View Name** field and accept the default option of **SummaryExample**.

9. Now we need to put debits and credits in the right order:

      ° Click on the expansion button (blue arrow) next to **List**

      ° Select **Debit Amount**

      ° Click **Move Up** to move **Debit Amount** ahead of **Credit Amount**

      ° Click **OK**

Note that you can change the name of the field in the **Display Name** column. This is the name that will be passed to Excel 2013.

The basic report setup is done. Let's look at some optional items including **Restrictions, Calculations**, and **Options**.

Restrictions

Restrictions allow you to limit the data sent to Excel. For example, you may want to limit the data to a specific year, certain territories, or a single department. To set up a basic restriction limiting the data to 2013:

1. Click on the **Restrictions** button and select the plus symbol **(+)** to add a restriction.

2. Set the restrictions as follows, then click **Save** and **OK**:

    ○ Table: **Account Summary Master View**
    ○ Field: **Year**
    ○ Restriction: **Is Equal To**
    ○ Value: **2013**

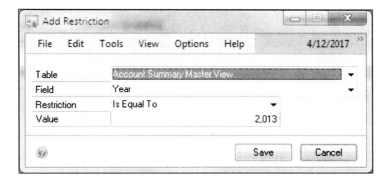

Calculations

You can perform basic calculations with Excel Report Builder. As an example, we'll subtract credit amount from debit amount. To demonstrate a simple calculation:

1. Click **Calculations** and pick the plus symbol **(+)** to add a calculation.

2. In **Field Name**, type `Difference` and set **Field Type** to **Currency**.

3. Click on the plus symbol (**+**) next to **Account Summary Master View**.
4. Scroll down and double-click **Debit Amount**.
5. Type the minus symbol (**-**) and double-click **Credit Amount**.
6. Click **Validate** to ensure that you did it right followed by **Save** and **Ok**.

Options

Finally, we have some options. Since we've only got one sample company to play with, we'll briefly talk about the **Options** button.

 We are talking about the **Options** button at the top of the screen in this section. There is also an **Options** menu item that provides the ability to duplicate Excel Report Builder reports, display the underlying SQL, and make bulk edits to field settings.

The **Options** button provides these selections:

- **Display totals at the end of each list**: This self-explanatory checkbox adds totals to the end of appropriate columns.
- **Multicompany report**: Create a multi-company report with data from multiple GP companies. When this is checked, you'll be able to choose which GP 2013 companies to report from. There are some additional multi-company options including:

- ○ **Consolidate all reports into a single workbook**: When an Excel report runs with this option, all companies export to a single workbook, but each company exports to its own worksheet with its own tab.

    If you choose **Consolidate all reports into a single workbook**, you can also choose **Create summary page** to create a consolidated summary tab.

- ○ **Consolidate all reports into a single worksheet**: This consolidates all companies into one worksheet. A summary page is not an option with this selection.

[If you're wondering about the Drill Down buttons, they are incredibly cool so they get their own chapter later.]

Publish

When you've got the Excel report the way you want it, click **Publish** to create the report. When you click **Publish**, the **Publish Report** window will open. To finish publishing:

1. Set **Report Type** to **Excel Report**.

2. Look up the **Report ID** with the magnifying glass icon and select **Summary Example**.

3. Choose **Publish To: File**.

4. Accept the default **Filename** as **Summary Example** under **Data Connection**.

5. Use the folder icon in the **Data Connection** section and look up the location where you deployed Excel reports. I'm using `C:\GP2013XL\ Data Connections\TWO\Financial\` to put this in the financial data connections folder.

6. Check the **Create Excel Report** box.

7. Accept the default **Excel Report** name as **Summary Example**.

8. Use the folder icon on the right in the **Create Excel Report** section and look up the location where you deployed Excel reports. I'm using `C:\GP2013XL\Reports\TWO\Financial\` to put this in the financial reports folder.

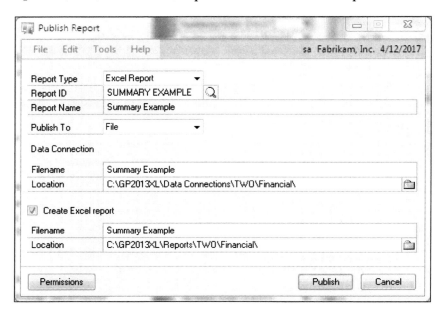

9. Click **Permissions** and review or adjust the roles that will have permission to this Excel report. Note that this simply adds this report to the selected SQL Server roles.

10. Click **Publish** to finish.

To publish an Excel report, you'll need to be either:

- The `sa` user
- The `DYNSA` user
- A user with the `db_owner` database role in SQL Server
- A user with the `sysadmin` fixed server role in SQL Server
- A user with the `dbcreator` fixed server role in SQL Server

We've worked through an example of creating an Excel report, but this example is by no means comprehensive. The SmartList builder manual included with Dynamics GP 2013 includes extensive coverage of Excel Report Builder. With Dynamics GP 2013, the manual has moved to the web at `http://download. microsoft.com/download/6/1/6/616FF1A6-9269-4A0B-83F8-D9024AA39FA5/ SmartListBuilderUsersGuide.pdf`. (short link: `http://bit.ly/X2Pn1t`)

Summary

We've looked at one of the best methods for getting data for our dashboard. We've deployed, secured, run, and built Excel reports. Now that we've thoroughly explored one of the best ways to get real-time data out of Dynamics GP 2013 and into Microsoft Excel, let's start looking at how to use this information as the foundation for a dashboard.

In the next chapter we will start to build our dashboard using one of the fundamental building blocks—pivot tables.

3
Pivot Tables: The Basic Building Blocks

Pivot tables are the basic building blocks of analysis in Excel. Almost any dashboard will incorporate pivot tables or pivot table-like functionality as part of its core. At their simplest, pivot tables let you group and summarize data in different ways to provide interesting views of data. At their most complex, they provide nearly infinite ways to analyze and visualize data. We can't fit an infinite number of ways in this book, so we'll use some common scenarios here.

In this chapter we will start building our Dynamics GP dashboard by learning about:

- Creating pivot tables from GP 2013 Excel report data
- Creating pivot tables from GP 2013 data connections
- Copying pivot tables
- Creating connected pivots tables from Excel
- Creating Excel Report Builder pivot tables
- Creating Power View reports

Throughout the course of this book, we're going to build a dashboard that looks like the one in the following screenshot, and we're going to use pivot tables as the foundation:

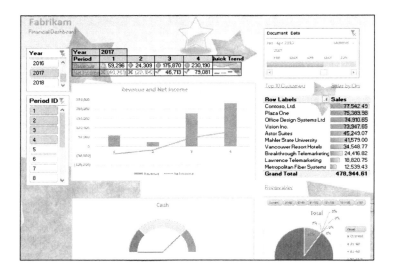

 The term "pivot table" is a generic term. Microsoft has trademarked the term "PivotTable", so you'll use the items in Excel labeled that way.

Creating pivot tables from GP 2013 Excel report data

The starting point for pivot tables is simply to use data in Microsoft Excel 2013. Pivot tables are one of those Excel features that remain a mystery for many people but are really very easy to use. In fact, their ease of use often disguises how powerful pivot tables really are.

Getting data to Excel

To build our first pivot table, let's start with the Two Account SummaryDefault Excel report that we used in *Chapter 2, The Ultimate GP to Excel Tool: Refreshable Excel Reports*.

1. In Dynamics GP, on the Navigation Pane on the left, click **Financial**. The List Pane above will change to show financial items.

2. In the List Pane, click **Excel Reports**.

3. In the Navigation List in the center, select **TWO AccountSummary Default**. Make sure that you select items where the **Option** includes **Reports**.

4. Double-click the **TWO AccountSummary Default** item.

5. In *Chapter 2, The Ultimate GP to Excel Tool: Refreshable Excel Reports*, we looked at how to turn off the Excel 2013 security warning at the top of the worksheet. If that still appears, click **Enable Content** and then circle back to the security section in the previous chapter. I'm assuming that you've got this fixed now, so we won't revisit it again.

Building a pivot table

Follow these steps to build the pivot table:

1. Use your cursor to select any cell in the table of data from the Excel report that you just brought into Dynamics GP.

2. Select **Insert | Pivot Table** from the Excel 2013 ribbon.

3. **Select a table or range** should be marked and the **Table/Range** should be **Table_AccountSummary_Default**:

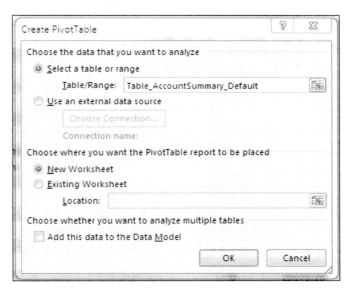

4. Notice that under **Choose where you want the PivotTable report to be placed**, we are putting this in a new worksheet. Click **OK**.

5. A new worksheet will open with the framework for a new pivot table report. In the **PivotTable Fields** box on the right, use your mouse to drag items into the areas at the bottom. Drag:

   ° **Year** to **Rows**
   ° **Period Balance** to **Values**
   ° **Account Number** to **Filters**
   ° **Period ID** to **Columns**

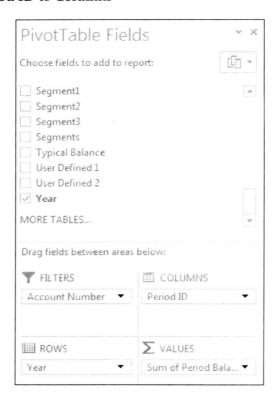

6. On the left, Excel 2013 will start building a pivot table by summarizing period balances for each year across periods. In the pivot table on the left, right-click and select **Expand/Collapse | Collapse Entire Field** to completely roll up the data.

7. This covers all the accounts. Let's just analyze one account for now. At the top of the PivotTable next to **Account Number**, change **(All)** to **000-1100-00**:

Account Number	000-1100-00	.T				
Sum of Period Balance	**Column Labels** ▾					
Row Labels ▾	**0**	**1**	**2**	**3**	**4**	**5**
2013	338562.25	40751.99	117.65			28000
2014	338562.25	241957.41	117.65			28000
2015		-19223.54				812.99
2016			55699.93	70493.94	233541.45	5279.5
2017			53588.83	-63272.47	172764.13	-50
Grand Total	677124.5	263485.86	109524.06	7221.47	406305.58	62042.49

That's it. You've built a pivot table. It's really that easy. Now we're ready to move into some more building blocks.

Creating pivot tables from GP 2013 data connections

One problem with creating a pivot table from data in Excel 2013 is that we have to bring the data from Dynamics GP 2013 into Microsoft Excel. That's not much of a burden when we're dealing with a few hundred rows, but when you get to transactional data, it's easy to have a couple of hundred thousand rows. This is where pivot table performance starts to bog down. For companies with a lot of accounts, high transaction volume, and a lot of history, it's easy to exceed Excel's maximum row count of 1,048,576 rows. Microsoft Excel 2013 lets us build pivot tables without having to bring the data into Excel.

When we deployed Dynamics GP 2013's Excel reports, we also deployed the data connectors. The connectors let us use data in Dynamics GP to build pivot tables without having to bring detailed data into Excel 2013. Let's use this to start to build our dashboard. For much of the rest of the book, you'll want to save the file that we're working with. It will ultimately grow into our dashboard. To build a pivot table from Dynamics GP without having to bring everything into Excel:

1. Close Excel 2013; we want a fresh start.
2. In Dynamics GP 2013, on the Navigation Pane on the left, click **Financial**. The List Pane above will change to show financial items.
3. In the List Pane, click **Excel Reports**.

4. In the Navigation List in the center, select **TWO AccountSummary**. This is a little different than last time. Make sure that you select the **Option** that includes **Data Connections**.

5. Double-click the **TWO AccountSummary** item.

6. Excel 2013 will open asking you what to do with the data. Despite also being named **Account Summary**, this connector is a little different. The **AccountSummary Default** report is actually a limited subset of data from the **AccountSummary** view. The AccountSummary connector has everything in the view so there is a lot more data available.

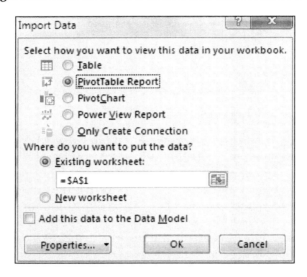

7. Select **PivotTable Report** and click **OK**.

Building a revenue pivot table

Now we have the framework for a pivot table again, but this time it's based on Dynamics GP data contained in SQL Server, not on data that we've brought into Excel. This also makes the Excel files much smaller.

Let's use this data to build a revenue pivot table for our dashboard:

1. Drag **Account Number** into **Rows**.

2. Drag **Account Category** into **Filters**.

3. Drag **Year** and **Period ID** into **Columns** with **Year** on top.

4. Drag **Period Balance** into **Values**.

5. Click the drop-down box on the **Account Category** filter at the top of the pivot table next to **(All)**.

6. Check the box marked **Select Multiple Items**.

7. Uncheck **(All)**.

8. Scroll down and check **Sales** and **Sales Returns and Discounts**:

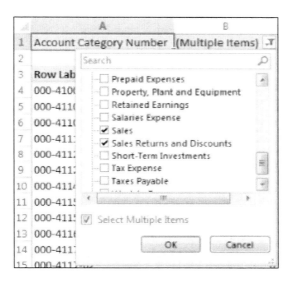

9. Select cell B4. This should contain the year 2013. To filter this to only show 2017, select the drop-down box next to **Column Labels**.

10. Uncheck **Select All** and check **2017**.

11. Select cell B5. This should now contain period **1**. To filter this to only show the first four months of 2017, select the drop-down box next to **Column Labels**.

12. Uncheck **Select All** and check periods **1** through **4**.

13. Finally, let's clean things up. Select cell H4, the **Grand Total** header. Right-click and select **Remove Grand Total**.

14. Select cells B6 through G10 and pick the comma style (,) from the **Number** section of the ribbon. Resize the columns as necessary.

	A	B	C	D	E
1	Account Category Number	(Multiple Items) .Y			
2					
3	**Sum of Amount**	Column Labels .Y			
4		⊟2017			
5	**Row Labels** ▾	**1**	**2**	**3**	**4**
6	000-4100-00	-	-	539.55	8,792.14
7	000-4110-01	3,799.00	-	2,659.30	579.65
8	000-4110-02	55,497.10	24,308.85	172,251.95	220,818.15
9	000-4140-00	-	-	419.40	-
10	**Grand Total**	**59,296.10**	**24,308.85**	**175,870.20**	**230,189.94**

Most of the time Excel formatting from the ribbon works fine, but every so often you'll get a pivot table that refuses to hold formatting even though others, just like it, work fine. I'm sure that someone will try to tell me that I'm crazy but it happened to a user this week while I was standing over them. The fix is typically to right-click on the pivot table and use the fonts and formatting options in the pivot table to format the data.

15. Right-click on the tab at the bottom of the worksheet, select **Rename**, and type `Revenue`.

16. Right-click in the pivot table and select **PivotTable Options**. Name the pivot table `Revenue`.

17. Save the file as `GP 2013 Dashboard.xlsx`. Make sure to save it somewhere that you can find it. We're going to continue working with this file. Saving here is just a precaution.

We've now built the source for the revenue data in our dashboard. This will also become our drill-back to the account numbers to support our revenue total.

Copying pivot tables

We have a pivot table for revenue, but we really need similar information to display net income on our dashboard. Fortunately, we don't have to go through that whole exercise again. Since our net income pivot table is based on the same data as our revenue pivot table, we can copy and paste. To create a net income-based pivot table:

1. Click anywhere inside the pivot table on the **Revenue** tab.
2. Select the **Analyze** tab under the **PivotTable Tools** grouping.
3. Click **Select | Entire PivotTable**.
4. Right-click in the pivot table and select **Copy**.
5. Create a new sheet using the plus (**+**) key at the bottom.
6. In cell A1, click on the **Paste** button on the **Home** ribbon.

Building the income pivot table

This creates a copy of the sheet on a different tab. Now we're ready to modify our copied pivot table.

1. Select the copied pivot table and drag **Account Category** off of the **Filter** area and back into the **PivotTable Fields** list.
2. Drag **Posting Type** into the **Filter** area:

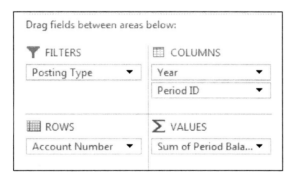

3. Open the drop-down box for the **Posting Type** filter next to **(All)** and select **Profit** and **Loss**.

4. We need to reset the periods to only show the first four. Select cell B5 and click the filter button next to **Column Labels**.

5. Uncheck **Select All** and check only periods **1** through **4**.

6. Rename the tab **Net Income**.

7. Right-click in the pivot table and select **PivotTable Options**. Name the pivot table Net Income.

8. Save the file.

	A	B	C	D	E	F
1	Posting Type	Profit and Loss				
2						
3	Sum of Period Balance	Column Labels				
4		2017				2017 Total
5	Row Labels	1	2	3	4	
6	000-4100-00			(539.55)	(8,792.14)	(9,331.69)
7	000-4110-01	(3,799.00)		(2,659.30)	(579.65)	(7,037.95)
8	000-4110-02	(55,497.10)	(24,308.85)	(172,251.95)	(220,818.15)	(472,876.05)
9	000-4140-00			(419.40)		(419.40)
10	000-4510-01	29,272.62	12,093.06	91,227.81	111,630.94	244,224.43
11	000-4600-00		(1.60)	(89.90)	(23.94)	(115.44)
12	000-5100-00	63,045.68	28,147.81	29,141.84	29,019.39	149,354.72
13	100-5150-00	1,431.65	1,430.24	1,432.12	1,431.83	5,725.84
14	100-5170-00	900.00	393.93	408.41	406.60	2,108.94
15	200-5170-00	3,848.23	1,684.56	1,746.19	1,738.60	9,017.58
16	300-5130-00	1,778.92	729.29	5,276.16	6,905.75	14,690.12
17	500-6150-00			15.00		15.00
18	Grand Total	40,981.00	20,168.44	(46,712.57)	(79,080.77)	(64,643.90)

We now have source data for two of the five major elements of our dashboard. And we can refresh this data any time from within Excel simply by selecting **Data | Refresh All**.

Creating a cash pivot table

We need a couple more pivot tables to round out our dashboard, so let's build them really fast. First we need cash, and since it's built from our account summary data as well, it makes this easy. For cash, we just want to see total cash. To build the cash pivot make another copy of the **Revenue** pivot table with these steps:

1. Click anywhere inside the pivot table on the **Revenue** tab.

2. Select the **Analyze** tab under the **PivotTable Tools** grouping.

3. Click **Select | Entire PivotTable**.

4. Right-click in the pivot table and select **Copy**.
5. Create a new sheet using the plus (**+**) key at the bottom.
6. In cell A1 click on the **Paste** button on the **Home** ribbon.
7. Rename the **Cash** tab.

Now let's modify it to just get the cash total:

1. In the **PivotTable Field List** area on the right:
   - Remove **Year** and **Period ID** from **Columns**
   - Remove **Accounts** from **Rows**
   - Move **Account Category Number** to **Rows**
   - Add **Year** to **Filters**

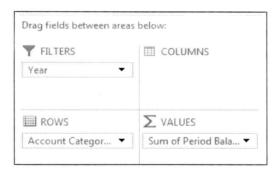

2. Select the filter symbol next to **Year** and check **(All)**.
3. Select the filter symbol next to **Row Labels** and uncheck everything except **Cash**.
4. Right-click in the pivot table and select **PivotTable Options**. Name the pivot table Cash.
5. Save the file.

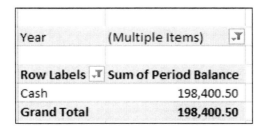

Year	(Multiple Items)
Row Labels	**Sum of Period Balance**
Cash	198,400.50
Grand Total	**198,400.50**

Nice job. We'll use this information as part of Speedometer graph later on.

 This works in the sample company because of the number of open years in the GP 2013 sample data. In the real world, you would typically only need the open year since it has a beginning balance and subsequent transactions.

Creating connected pivot tables from inside Excel

So far we've created pivot tables by starting in Dynamics GP 2013 and sending information to Excel. We can also use Excel 2013 to pull data out of Dynamics GP. For our dashboard, we need some sales data and receivables totals. The sales data that we want exists as a Dynamics GP data connection. The receivables data connection doesn't contain quite what we need, so we'll have to adjust it.

Building the sales pivot table

Let's add a sales pivot table first. To create our sales pivot table:

1. In Excel 2013, click plus (+) next to the worksheet tabs 2013 to add a new worksheet. Name the worksheet `Top Ten Customers`.

2. Select the **Data** tab and click **Existing Connections** from the ribbon.

3. Click **Browse for More** and navigate to where you installed the GP 2013 data connections for the sample company. Earlier we deployed this to `C:\GP2013XL\Data Connections\TWO`.

4. Select the **Sales** directory and double-click **TWO SalesTransactions Posted Invoices**.

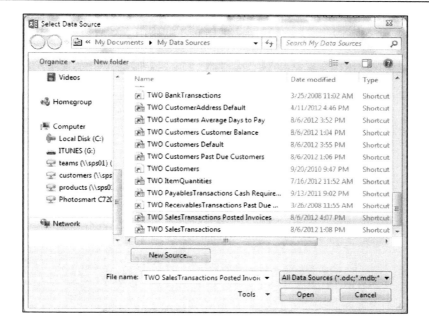

5. The **Import Data** window will open. Select **PivotTable Report** and click **OK**.

6. Click in the pivot table framework area to bring up the **PivotTable Field List** on the right.

7. Drag **Customer Name** into **Rows**.

8. Drag **Document Amount** into **Values**.

We don't need all of our customers' sales; that's too much information for a dashboard. Let's limit it to the top 10 customers by sales. To show only the top 10 customers:

1. Click on the first customer name in the sales pivot table.

2. Right-click and select **Filter | Top 10**.

3. Notice that we're not limited to the top or just to ten items, but this is good enough for now, so click **OK**.

4. To sort the sales from highest to lowest, select an amount field in the pivot table. On the **Home** tab, select **Sort & Filter, Sort Largest to Smallest**:

2		
3	**Row Labels** ⭷	**Sum of Document Amount**
4	Plaza One	159,211.89
5	Mahler State University	94,697.45
6	Vancouver Resort Hotels	93,235.36
7	Lawrence Telemarketing	93,105.17
8	Astor Suites	91,846.69
9	Contoso, Ltd.	82,667.53
10	Office Design Systems Ltd	74,910.65
11	Vision Inc.	73,947.65
12	Breakthrough Telemarketing	47,321.46
13	Aaron Fitz Electrical	25,171.60
14	**Grand Total**	**836,115.45**
15		

 Like formatting, if sorting doesn't stick when refreshing a pivot table, right-click in the pivot table and use the **Sort** option instead.

5. Highlight everything in the **Sum of Document Amount** column and click the comma (,) in the **Number** section of the **Home** tab on the ribbon. This formats the amounts as Accounting with no currency symbol.

6. Right-click in the pivot table and select **PivotTable Options**. Name the pivot table `Top 10 Customers`.

7. Save the file.

Adding a receivables pivot table

Now our pivot table has been reduced to just the top 10 customers by sales and ordered appropriately. All that is left for our foundation is adding receivables aging. To add receivables:

1. In Excel 2013, click plus (+) next to the worksheet tabs to add a new worksheet. Name the worksheet as `Receivables Aging`.
2. Select the **Data** tab and click **Existing Connections** from the ribbon.
3. Click **Browse for More** and navigate to where you installed the GP 2013 data connections for the sample company. Earlier we installed this in `C:\GP2013XL\Data Connections\TWO`.
4. Select the **Sales** directory and double-click **TWO Customers Past Due Customers**.
5. The **Import Data** window will open.
6. We need to modify the data coming in, so click on **Properties | Definition**.

This view holds past due customer amounts. We want all customer amounts, not just past due totals, so we have to remove the limitation on this data.

1. In the **Command Text** window, scroll down to the word **where**. Highlight the word **where** with your mouse and select all the rest of the text:

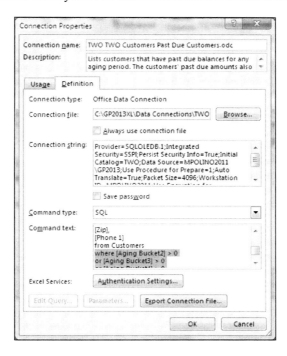

2. Press *Delete* to remove the restrictions. Click **OK** to the message that this workbook will no longer match the file and click **OK** to continue.

3. Select **PivotTable Report** and click **OK**.

4. Click in the pivot table framework area to bring up the **PivotTable Field List** on the right.

5. Drag each one of the **Aging Buckets** down into **Values**.

6. Drag **Values** from the **Columns** area to **Rows**:

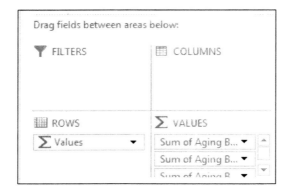

7. Right-click in the pivot table and select **PivotTable Options**. Name the pivot table Receivables Aging.

8. Save the file.

Now that we have the data foundation of our dashboard completed, let's look at a couple of other options for when you build your own dashboard.

Excel Report Builder pivot tables

In *Chapter 2*, *The Ultimate GP to Excel Tool: Refreshable Excel Reports*, we looked at building our own refreshable Excel reports using Excel Report Builder. In that process we brought data from Microsoft Dynamics GP 2013 into Excel. But here we've seen how powerful pivot tables can be without forcing the data to reside in Microsoft Excel 2013.

Along the way we've also found that, even though Dynamics GP 2013 has some great Excel reports, sometimes we need to adjust the information being brought over by those reports. Finally, people often want to build additional analyses without having to adjust the data each time. Fortunately, Excel Report Builder offers a way to deliver connected pivot tables instead of just lists of data. In this section we'll look at how to build a pivot table report using Excel Report Builder.

To use Excel Report Builder to create a pivot table:

1. Open Microsoft Dynamics GP 2013 and navigate to **Microsoft Dynamics GP | Tools | SmartList Builder | Excel Report Builder | Excel Report Builder**.

2. Use the lookup button next to **Report ID** to find the **Summary Example** report that we created in *Chapter 2, The Ultimate GP to Excel Tool: Refreshable Excel Reports*.

3. Change the **Report Type** from **List** to **Pivot Table**.

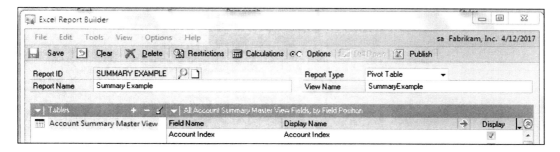

4. Click **Publish**.

Because this report has already been published once (we did it in *Chapter 2, The Ultimate GP to Excel Tool: Refreshable Excel Reports*), the information should be filled in and all you should have to do is verify that the details are correct. If you were publishing this for the first time you would need to perform all the following steps. Since we've done this already, just confirm the information here.

5. Set **Report Type** to **Excel Report**.

6. Look up the **Report ID** with the magnifying glass icon and select **Summary Example**.

7. Select **Publish To: File**.

8. Accept the default data connection **Filename** of **Summary Example**.

9. Use the folder icon in the **Data Connection** section and look up the location where you deployed Excel reports. In this case we are using C:\GP2013XL\Data Connections\TWO\Financial\ to put this in the financial data connections folder.

10. Check the **Create Excel Report** box.

11. Accept the default Excel Report name of **Summary Example**.

12. Use the folder icon in the Excel Report section and look up the location where you deployed Excel reports. I'm using `C:\GP2013XL\Reports\TWO\Financial\` to put this in the financial reports folder.

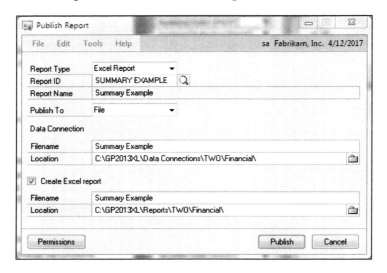

To run this pivot table-based Excel report:

1. Select **Financial** from the Navigation Pane on the left.

2. Select **Excel Reports** from the list above.

3. Scroll down in the center section and double-click **TWO Summary Example**.

4. Excel will open with the framework for a pivot table and the **PivotTable Field** list is ready for you to start building:

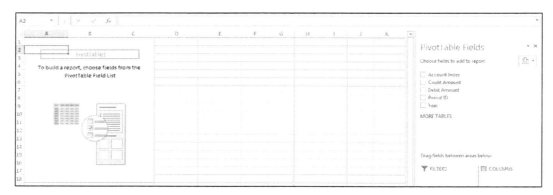

Creating Power View reports

Power View is a new data visualization tool built into Microsoft Excel 2013. At its core it behaves like a pivot table, so whether Microsoft technically calls it a pivot table or not, we're going to cover it here.

Power View reports exist on their own sheet and they can't be copied and pasted into traditional Excel sheets. So what are they good for? Well, you can do some crazy things with Power View, and it may ultimately become a great primary dashboard tool. Even though we're not going to roll it into our dashboard right now, we will set it up as a link from the main dashboard. You might also show it off to get some support for building your own dashboard.

Power View reports make great executive eye candy. For our scenario, we want to see sales by city and state in the U.S. While a pivot table could do this, a Power View map is so much cooler.

To build our Power View map:

1. Select the **Data** tab and click **Existing Connections** from the ribbon.
2. Click **Browse for More** and navigate to where you installed the GP 2013 data connections for the sample company. Earlier we put this in `C:\GP2013XL\ Data Connections\TWO`.
3. Select the **Sales** directory and double-click **TWO SalesTransactions**.
4. The **Import Data** window will open. Select **Power View Report** and click **OK**:

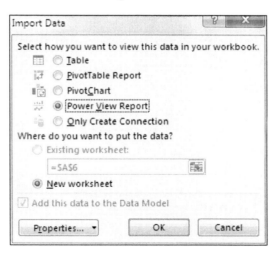

5. You'll see that the screen looks a lot like the pivot table screen that we've been working with.

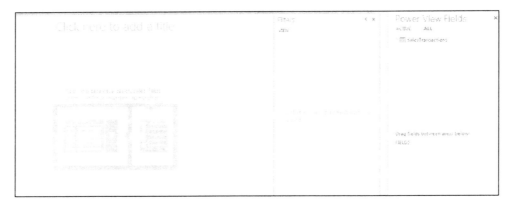

6. Select **SalesTransactions** on the right and click the down arrow to expand it.

7. Drag these fields from under **SalesTransactions** into the **Fields** box below in the following order:

   ° **State**

   ° **City**

   ° **Document Amount**

8. Power View will start to build a pivot table on the left.

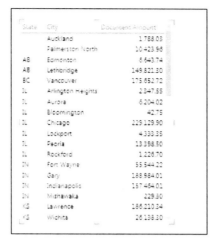

9. Drag **Country** into the **Filters** section and check **USA**:

So far, so good. We have a nice pivot table with sales per city for the U.S., but it's not much different from the pivot tables we've been building. Here is where the payoff comes.

10. Select the **Design** tab and click **Map**. Power View creates a small map in place of the pivot table.

11. Hover your mouse over the map and click the pop-out icon. The icon is a right angle with an outward-facing arrow. The map expands to show the U.S.. Colored circles indicate cities with sales. Larger circles indicate higher dollar amounts:

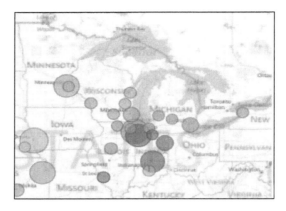

12. Use the plus (**+**) and minus (**-**) keys, or your mouse's scroll wheel, to zoom and expand the map. Drag the map around with your mouse to reposition it. You can even use your finger if you are using a touchscreen.

13. Rename the tab **Sales by City** and save the worksheet.

Our map isn't perfect. Because it's only using city for location, it places Woodbury, Minnesota in Tennessee. A combined city/state field can produce better results but I think you get the idea of how useful a Power View map can be.

We are just scratching the surface of Power View. Power View maps can use latitude and longitude data for improved precision. You can have multiple elements such as pivot tables, graphs, charts, and more on a single Power View window. I won't be surprised to see Power View eventually have whole books dedicated to its feature set. Since this isn't a Power View book, I'll leave this for you to explore more on your own.

Summary

We've built a pile of pivot tables in this chapter and we've done it using almost every scenario possible. This is great practice for when you start building a dashboard for your organization. We're not done with pivot tables yet. Near the end of the book, we look at turbo charging pivot tables with PowerPivot.

In the next chapter, we will start to build the look and feel of our dashboard with conditional formatting. This is another key element, and it's a big part of making a dashboard look great.

4
Making Things Pretty with Formatting and Conditional Formatting

Now that we have our data elements for a dashboard, we'll start to pull the pieces together and format them. The stereotype is that accountants care more about the numbers than about presentation. The stereotype misses the point, as do some accountants. The point is to present the numbers in a way that they can be clearly understood. Burying important data in a long, ugly list of numbers is an accounting sin. So is hiding poor financial results by surrounding them with upbeat photos in an annual report. Both methods are attempts to hide the truth. With our dashboard, we are trying to present information in a way that makes it easy to understand and discover new insights. In this chapter we will start assembling and formatting our dashboard using:

- Get Pivot Data
- Excel formatting
- Icon sets
- Data bars
- Color Scales
- Other formatting

The idea behind conditional formatting is that we want data elements to change visually based on the value of the data. The simplest example is the classic way of presenting positive numbers in black and negative numbers in red. With the conditional formatting options in Excel we can do so much more. But first, we have to start building our dashboard.

 The presentation of negative numbers in red is where we get the English phrase "in the red" to describe a company that is losing money.

Recap

As a reminder, we are working to build a dashboard that looks like this:

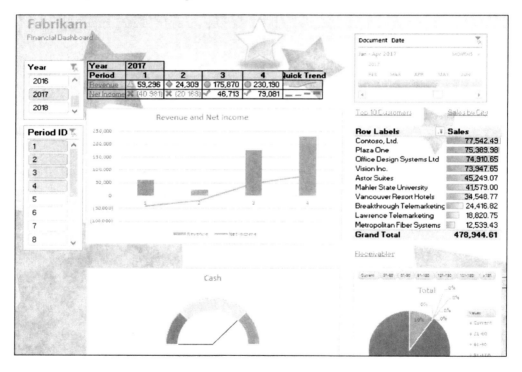

Through the first three chapters we learned how to get data from Microsoft Dynamics GP 2013 into Excel 2013. Along the way we built a set of pivot tables to serve as the source data for our dashboard. This chapter is where we start to see the dashboard take shape.

Preparation

The idea behind any financial dashboard is to give users a snapshot of key business metrics. On a car dashboard, more important information is given greater weight; that is, the gauges are bigger, placed in the center, and so on. Periodically important data is highlighted as necessary, like when the low fuel light comes on to ensure that you are paying attention to the fuel gauge. It doesn't hurt to think that way for financial dashboards as well. We don't want to clutter up our dashboard with too much information.

Now that we have the data that we need, we need to set up a sheet to hold our dashboard. To create a new sheet:

1. Open the `GP 2013 Dashboard.xlsx` file that we saved in the previous chapter.
2. On the bottom of the sheet to the right of the tabs, click on the plus (**+**) button to create a new sheet.
3. Use the left mouse button to drag the new sheet all the way to the left, making it the first sheet on the left.
4. Right-click on the sheet name and select **Rename**.
5. Rename the sheet as `Dashboard`.

Now that we have a place to build our dashboard, let's get started.

Get Pivot Data

We want revenue and net income information on our dashboard, but they live in two different pivot tables in our data. Plus, there is more information in those pivot tables than we want on our dashboard. The answer to this is—Microsoft's **Get Pivot Data** formula. Fortunately, you don't really need to spend much time figuring how to use the formula. Let's set up revenue and net income on our dashboard. To do this:

1. In cell D5 of the **Dashboard** sheet, type `Year`.
2. In cell D6, type `Period`.

3. In cell D7, type `Revenue`.

4. In cell D8, type `Net Income`.

	A	B	C	D	E
1					
2					
3					
4					
5				Year	
6				Period	
7				Revenue	
8				Net Income	
9					

Revenue

As a reminder, our revenue pivot table looks like this:

	A	B	C	D	E
1	Account Category Number	(Multiple Items) ⊽			
2					
3	**Sum of Amount**	**Column Labels** ⊽			
4		⊟2017			
5	**Row Labels** ▾	1	2	3	4
6	000-4100-00	-	-	539.55	8,792.14
7	000-4110-01	3,799.00	-	2,659.30	579.65
8	000-4110-02	55,497.10	24,308.85	172,251.95	220,818.15
9	000-4140-00	-	-	419.40	-
10	**Grand Total**	59,296.10	24,308.85	175,870.20	230,189.94

Now that we have our heading information, let's add revenue and expense data:

1. Select cell E5 on the **Dashboard** sheet.

2. Type the equal sign (=) to start an Excel formula.

3. With your mouse, select the **Revenue** tab.

4. Click on cell B4 on the **Revenue** worksheet. This should be the year value **2017**. Hit *Enter* when done.

◢	A	B	C	D	E
1					
2					
3					
4					
5				Year	2017
6				Period	
7				Revenue	
8				Net Income	
9					

You should now have **2017** sitting in cell E5 next to **Year**. To add periods:

1. Select cell E6 on the **Dashboard** sheet.
2. Type the equal sign (=) to start an Excel formula.
3. With your mouse, select the **Revenue** tab.
4. Click on cell B5 on the **Revenue** worksheet. This should be period **1**. Hit *Enter* when done.

 Because these are just filters and not pivot table results, we can copy them.

5. Right-click on cell E6 on the **Dashboard** sheet and select **Copy**.
6. With your mouse, highlight cells F6, G6, and H6.
7. Right-click and select **Paste**.

◢	A	B	C	D	E	F	G	H
1								
2								
3								
4								
5				Year	2017			
6				Period	1	2	3	4
7				Revenue				
8				Net Income				

Now that we have our year at the top and our periods, let's add some data.

1. On the **Dashboard** worksheet, select cell E7 and type in the equal sign (=).

2. Move to the **Revenue** worksheet, select cell B10, and press *Enter*.

This places the revenue amount for period **1** on the dashboard. If you highlight the amount, you'll see that the formula is a little strange. It looks like:

```
=GETPIVOTDATA("Amount",Revenue!$A$3,"Year","2017","Period ID",1)
```

This is telling Excel to get the `Amount` value from the pivot table that starts in cell A3 where year is `2017` and `Period ID` is `1`. That works great for this cell, but there are two problems with this formula. First, because 2017 and 1 are hardcoded, this formula won't adjust when you copy cells for period 2, period 3, and so on. For the same reason, if the pivot table is changed to a different year or to reflect different periods, our dashboard won't update. We need to improve this formula. To make the Get Pivot Data formula more flexible:

1. Select the formula in cell E7.

2. Highlight just **"2017"** in the formula (including the quotes), click on cell E5, press the *F4* key to add anchors (dollar signs), and hit *Enter*. The formula should now look like:

```
=GETPIVOTDATA("Amount",Revenue!$A$3,"Year",$E$5,"Period ID",1)
```

3. Highlight just the number **1** in the formula, click on cell E6, and key in a dollar sign ($) before the number 6 to anchor it. Hit *Enter* when done. The final formula should look like this:

```
=GETPIVOTDATA("Amount",Revenue!$A$3,"Year",$E$5,"Period ID",E$6)
```

4. Now you can copy the formula to cells F7, G7, and H7.

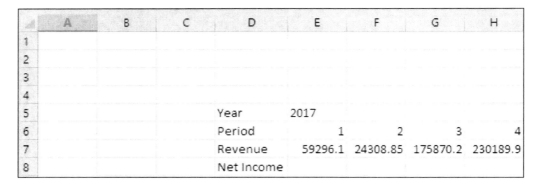

	A	B	C	D	E	F	G	H
1								
2								
3								
4								
5				Year	2017			
6				Period	1	2	3	4
7				Revenue	59296.1	24308.85	175870.2	230189.9
8				Net Income				

Net Income

We need to repeat this process to add net income. Our net income pivot table from *Chapter 3, Pivot Tables: The Basic Building Blocks,* looks like this:

	A	B	C	D	E	F
1	Posting Type	Profit and Loss				
2						
3	Sum of Period Balance	Column Labels				
4		⊟2017				2017 Total
5	Row Labels	1	2	3	4	
6	000-4100-00			(539.55)	(8,792.14)	(9,331.69)
7	000-4110-01	(3,799.00)		(2,659.30)	(579.65)	(7,037.95)
8	000-4110-02	(55,497.10)	(24,308.85)	(172,251.95)	(220,818.15)	(472,876.05)
9	000-4140-00			(419.40)		(419.40)
10	000-4510-01	29,272.62	12,093.06	91,227.81	111,630.94	244,224.43
11	000-4600-00		(1.60)	(89.90)	(23.94)	(115.44)
12	000-5100-00	63,045.68	28,147.81	29,141.84	29,019.39	149,354.72
13	100-5150-00	1,431.65	1,430.24	1,432.12	1,431.83	5,725.84
14	100-5170-00	900.00	393.93	408.41	406.60	2,108.94
15	200-5170-00	3,848.23	1,684.56	1,746.19	1,738.60	9,017.58
16	300-5130-00	1,778.92	729.29	5,276.16	6,905.75	14,690.12
17	500-6150-00			15.00		15.00
18	Grand Total	40,981.00	20,168.44	(46,712.57)	(79,080.77)	(64,643.90)

To get net income below revenue, follow these steps:

1. On the **Dashboard** worksheet, select cell E8 and type in the equal sign (=).

2. Move to the **Net Income** worksheet, select cell B18, and press *Enter*. This gives you a default formula of:

   ```
   =GETPIVOTDATA("Amount",'Net Income'!$A$3,"Year","2017","Period
   ID",1)
   ```

3. Select the formula in cell E8.

4. Highlight just **"2017"** in the formula, click on cell E5, press the *F4* key to add anchors ($), and hit *Enter*. The formula should now look like:

   ```
   =GETPIVOTDATA("Amount",'Net Income'!$A$3,"Year",$E$5,"Period
   ID",1)
   ```

5. Highlight just the number **1** in the formula, click on cell E6, and key a dollar sign ($) before the number **6** to anchor it. Hit *Enter* when done. The final formula should look like this:

   ```
   =GETPIVOTDATA("Amount",'Net Income'!$A$3,"Year",$E$5,"Period
   ID",E$6)
   ```

6. Now you can copy the formula to cells F8, G8, and H8.

	D	E	F	G	H
Year		2017			
Period		1	2	3	4
Revenue		59296.1	24308.85	175870.2	230189.9
Net Income		-40981	-20168.4	46712.57	79080.77

Formatting

Now that we have a start to our dashboard, let's improve the look of our revenue and net income table. To do this, follow these steps:

1. On the **Dashboard** sheet, select cells D5 and E5.

2. Right-click and select **Format Cells**.

3. On the **Font** tab, set **Font Style** to **Bold**.

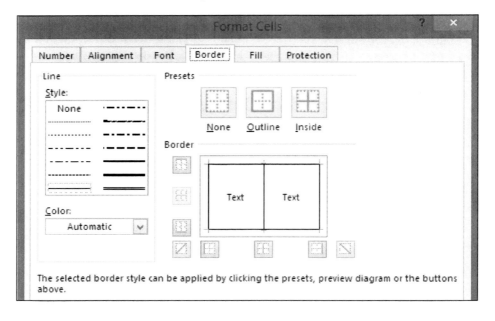

4. On the **Border** tab, click on the **Outline** and **Inside** buttons.

5. On the **Fill** tab, select a light gray background for these cells and hit *OK*.

6. Highlight cells D6 through H6.

7. Right-click and select **Format Cells**.

8. On the **Font** tab, set **Font Style** to **Bold**.

9. On the **Alignment** tab, set **Horizontal** to **Center**.

10. On the **Border** tab, click on the **Outline** and **Inside** buttons.

11. On the **Fill** tab, select a light gray background for these cells and hit *OK*.

D	E	F	G	H
Year	2017			
Period	1	2	3	4
Revenue	59296.1	24308.85	175870.2	230189.9
Net Income	-40981	-20168.4	46712.57	79080.77

12. Highlight cells D7 through H8.

13. Right-click and select **Format Cells**.

14. On the **Number** tab, set **Category** to `Number` and **Decimal places** to `0`.

15. Check the box next to **Use 1000 separator (,)**.

16. Under **Use Negative Numbers**, select the red numbers with parentheses:

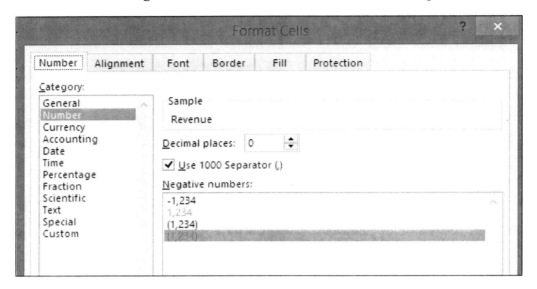

17. On the **Border** tab, click on the **Outline** and **Inside** buttons and hit *OK*.

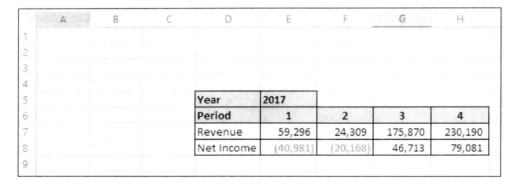

We put boxes around the data because at the end we are going to turn off gridlines in Excel. We want to highlight this data, not have it floating around in space. The lines help set this data off from other elements.

Now that we have the start of our dashboard, let's layer in some conditional formatting, starting with icon sets.

Icon sets

Icon sets are a great way to segregate data with an identifier based on thresholds. For example, we can say that any time revenue is above a certain number, we're doing fine. If it's between two numbers; we're worried, and below a certain number we're in trouble. Icon sets let you represent data like this graphically. A firm might say that monthly revenue over a million dollars is fine, revenue between 750,000 and a million is okay, and revenue under seven fifty requires management to intervene to find out what's going on.

The first tier can be represented by a green circle, the middle tier by a yellow triangle, and the last tier by a red diamond. This gives anyone even glancing at the dashboard a good idea of what needs their attention.

 An option in Excel 2013 is to use the same icon but a different color to represent the different tiers: a circle in red, yellow, or green, for example. This isn't a great idea for two reasons. First, some people have trouble distinguishing color. I worked for a color blind controller for a while and it made me appreciate the power of shapes. Second, the dashboard may get printed out for someone to take with them. If it's printed in black and white, the power of color is lost. I recommend that you use both symbols and color when using indicators.

You can also build icon sets based on any number of other criteria including percent, a formula or percentile rank. At I.B.I.S., we use icon sets to review consultant utilization status as a percentage. As a consultant, I really want to see a green checkmark by my name.

For our dashboard, we'll use a straightforward example:

Status	Revenue	Net income
Acceptable (green)	>6,000	>40,000
Concerned (yellow)	>25,000 and <60,000	>0 and <40,000
Requires Attention (red)	<25,000	<0

To set up our icon sets:

1. Select cells E7 through H7.
2. On the **Home** ribbon, select **Conditional Formatting | Icon Sets**.

3. Under **Shapes**, select the second option, which displays a green circle, a yellow triangle, and a red diamond:

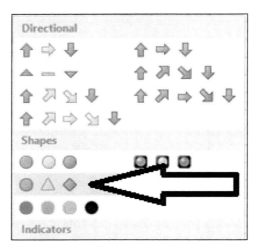

4. Back on the ribbon, select **Conditional Formatting | Manage Rules**.
5. Click on the **Edit Rules** button.

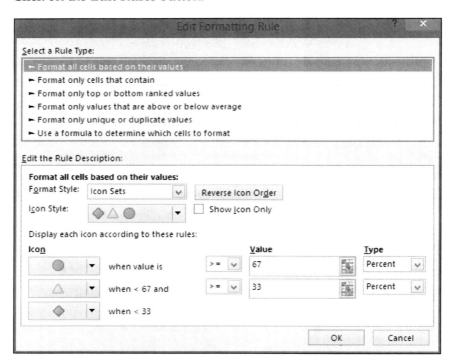

6. To the right of the green circle icon, change **Type** to **Number**.

7. Set **Value** equal to 60000.

8. To the right of the yellow triangle, change **Type** to **Number**.

9. Set **Value** equal to 25000 and click **OK**.

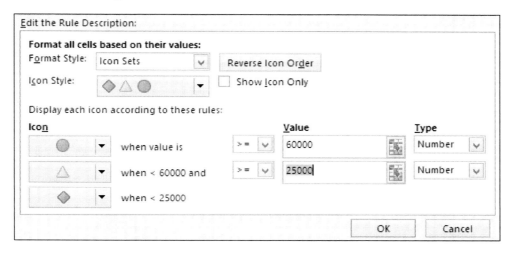

Now you should have icons next to the revenue amounts:

	A	B	C	D	E	F	G	H
1								
2								
3								
4								
5				Year	2017			
6				Period	1	2	3	4
7				Revenue	△ 59,296	◇ 24,309	● 175,870	● 230,190
8				Net Income	(40,981)	(20,168)	46,713	79,081

Let's do the same thing for net income:

1. Select cells E8 through H8.

2. On the **Home** ribbon, select **Conditional Formatting | Icon Sets**.

3. Under **Indicators**, select the first option on the right, which displays a green checkmark, a yellow exclamation mark, and a red X:

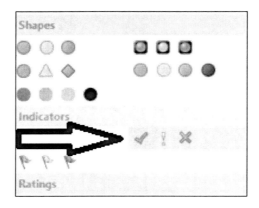

4. Back on the ribbon, select **Conditional Formatting | Manage Rules**.
5. Click on the **Edit Rules** button.
6. To the right of the green circle icon, change **Type** to **Number**.
7. Set **Value** equal to 40000.
8. To the right of the yellow triangle, change **Type** to **Number**.
9. Set **Value** equal to 0 and click **OK**.

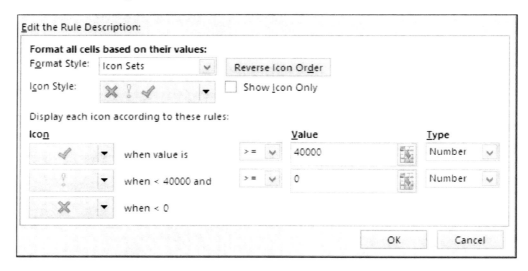

Now you should have revenue and net income with status indicators based on icon sets:

Year	2017			
Period	**1**	**2**	**3**	**4**
Revenue	△ 59,296	◇ 24,309	⬤ 175,870	⬤ 230,190
Net Income	✗ (40,981)	✗ (20,168)	✓ 46,713	✓ 79,081

 Normally, I wouldn't recommend mixing symbols like we do in this example. Mixing symbols is confusing to users. It's better to pick an icon set and stick with it, but I'm willing to break a rule or two to show off some cool options, and I think that this is a good time to break some rules.

Our initial formatting of negative numbers as red provided the bare minimum for conditional formatting. By adding in icon sets, we were able to give context to the numbers. Even though a number is positive, it doesn't mean that the number is acceptable. Icon sets are one tool that can be used to provide that additional information. Let's move on to some other tools, namely, color scales and data bars.

 Though there are arrows in the icon sets, the arrows don't necessarily represent a trend. They could be used, for example, to show amounts over or under a goal. You can use a formula and arrows to show the latest direction of change. An example is when newspapers put an up or down arrow next to a sports team based on their last performance. This typically includes something like "W3" and an up arrow to show three wins in a row and a positive indicator. To really show a trend, you're better off using Sparklines. We will cover Sparklines in a later chapter.

Data bars

Data bars are most often used to show how data points relate to each other. For example, earlier we created a pivot table with our top ten customers. It would be nice to know how much larger the top customer is when compared to the number ten customer. Data bars make this a very easy visualization to create without taking up additional space.

Let's add our top ten customers to our dashboard and create data bars to enhance the information. Since everything we need is in our pivot table, we don't have to use Get Pivot Table formulas. We can just copy our pivot table onto the dashboard.

To get our top ten customers on the dashboard:

1. On the **Dashboard** worksheet, select cell K10.

2. In cell K10, type `Top 10 Customers`. We'll use this later.

3. Select the **Top 10 Customers** tab.

4. Select cells A3 through B14. This should be the entire Top 10 Customers pivot table.

5. Right-click and select **Copy**.

6. Select the **Dashboard** worksheet.

7. Select cell K12, right-click, and select the leftmost paste icon. Hovering over this icon shows **Paste (p)** in the tip.

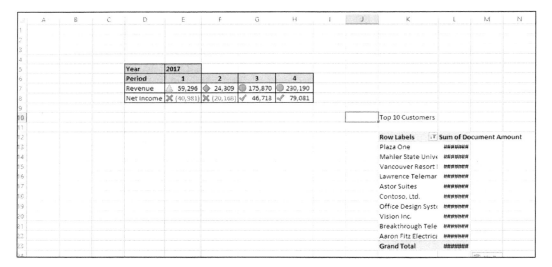

This will drop a copy of the Top 10 Customers pivot table on the dashboard. Now we need to clean it up and add data bars.

8. Use the handles at the top of cell K to widen the cell so that the data fits.

9. Select cell L12, **Sum of Documents**, and right-click.

10. Click **Value Field Settings**.

11. Change the **Custom Name** field from **Sum of Document Amount** to **Sales** and click **OK**:

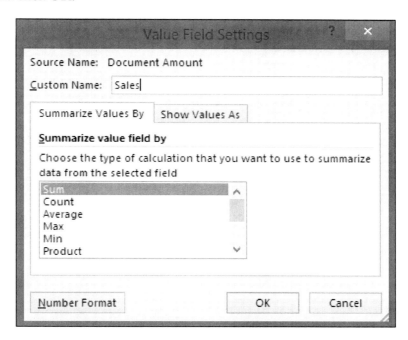

12. Highlight cells L13 through L23.

13. Right-click and select **Format Cells**.

14. On the **Number** tab, set **Category** to Number and **Decimal places** to 0.

15. Check the box next to **Use 1000 separator (,)**.

16. Under **Use Negative Numbers**, select the red numbers with parentheses.

17. Adjust the width of column **L** as necessary to ensure that all the numbers are shown properly:

Top 10 Customers	
Row Labels ⫟	**Sales**
Plaza One	159,212
Mahler State University	94,697
Vancouver Resort Hotels	93,235
Lawrence Telemarketing	93,105
Astor Suites	91,847
Contoso, Ltd.	82,668
Office Design Systems Ltd	74,911
Vision Inc.	73,948
Breakthrough Telemarketing	47,321
Aaron Fitz Electrical	25,172
Grand Total	**836,115**

Now let's add data bars. To do this:

1. Select cells L13 through L22. This is the sales column for Top 10 Customers without any headers or totals.

2. On the **Home** ribbon, select **Conditional Formatting | Data Bars**.

3. Under **Gradient Fill**, select the blue data bar.

4. Save the file.

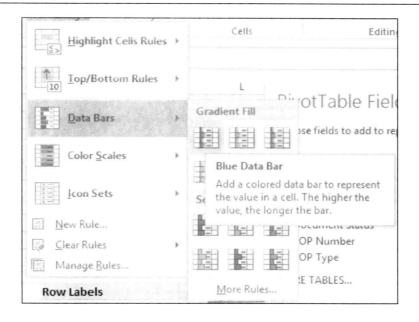

Blue data bars will appear inside the cells with sales numbers. Each bar represents how a customer's sales compare to the other top ten customers.

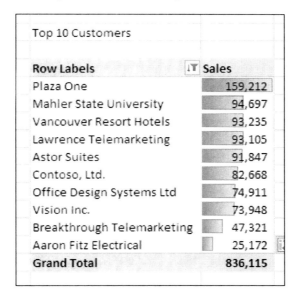

The sample company data visually shows that **Plaza One** has significantly higher sales than all the others. The next seven are relatively close, with a dramatic drop off for the ninth and tenth highest customers.

Visualizations like this can put a relationship into perspective. Clearly, the top eight customers should get the most attention. The difference between number eight and number two is pretty small. Just as clearly, **Plaza One** needs special attention because of its size. This data isn't yet limited by date. We'll tackle that when we get to slicers, so you'll get to see this information change before we are done.

 Data bars show the relationship against the other items in the data set, not against the total. For example, Mahler State University's value is roughly sixty percent of Plaza One's value and the bar is about sixty percent as long. There is a great, in-depth discussion of how data bars work at `http://blogs.office.com/b/microsoft-excel/archive/2009/08/07/data-bar-improvements-in-excel-2010.aspx`. (short link: http://bit.ly/Zn5zII)

Color Scales

Excel 2013 provides another conditional formatting option that is a kind of mix between icon sets and data bars. It's called **Color Scales**. Color Scales behave more like icon sets but are closer in appearance to data bars. We don't have a place for them on our main dashboard, but we do have a spot in some of the source pivot tables that we'll also use for drillbacks.

Let's see how Color Scales work. To set up Color Scales:

1. Select the **Revenue** worksheet.
2. Highlight cells B6 through E9.
3. From the **Home** ribbon, select **Conditional Formatting | Color Scales**.
4. Select the first Color Scale (**Green – Yellow – Red Color Scale**):

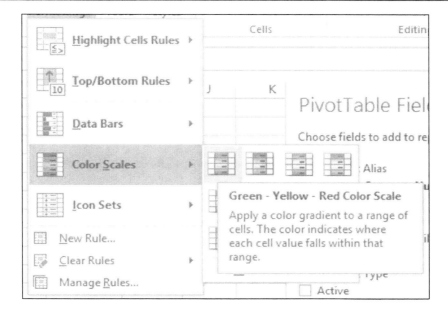

With this selection, Excel 2013 will automatically make the largest number green and the smallest number red, thus making it easy to see key highs and lows:

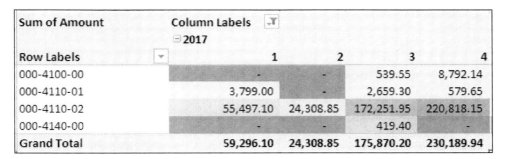

Sum of Amount	Column Labels			
	2017			
Row Labels	1	2	3	4
000-4100-00	-	-	539.55	8,792.14
000-4110-01	3,799.00	-	2,659.30	579.65
000-4110-02	55,497.10	24,308.85	172,251.95	220,818.15
000-4140-00	-	-	419.40	-
Grand Total	59,296.10	24,308.85	175,870.20	230,189.94

Adjusting Color Scales

To adjust the Color Scales, follow these steps:

1. Highlight cells B6 through E9.
2. From the **Home** ribbon, select **Conditional Formatting | Manage Rules**.

3. Click on the **Edit Rules** button.

4. Changing the **Midpoint** value adjusts the scale.

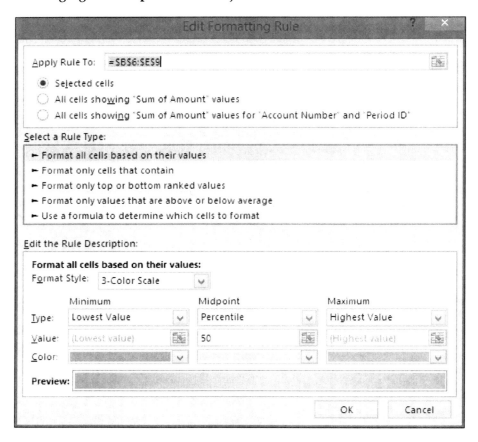

By default the lowest value is red, the highest value is green, the 50th percentile is yellow, and Excel scales the color for values in between. Lowering the **Midpoint** number increases the amount of green; increasing it produces more red.

The green/yellow/red limit

Now that you understand the concept of limits and green/yellow/red, we're going to do some setup along those lines to support a speedometer chart. We'll build the chart in the next chapter. A speedometer chart is surprisingly hard to create in Excel, so we're doing the pre-work here. This setup sets the green/yellow/red limits for that chart.

1. Select the **Cash** worksheet.

2. In cell D6 type `Cash`.

3. In cell E5 type `Actual`.

4. In cell F5 type `Meter use Only:`

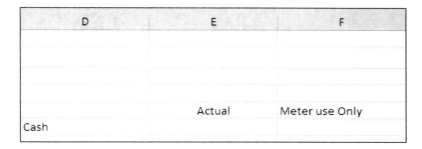

5. In cell E6, type the equal sign (=), the negative sign (-), and select cell B5. This is the cash amount from the pivot table. You should see a formula that looks like this:

    `=-GETPIVOTDATA("Amount",$A$4,"Account Category Number","Cash")`

6. In cell D9 type `Meter Level`.

7. In cell E9 type `Difference`.

8. In cells D10 through D12 type `Red`, `Yellow`, and `Green` respectively.

9. In cell E10 type `1000000`.

10. In cell E11 type `3000000`.

11. In cell E12 type `4000000`. These are the red, yellow, and green values.

12. In cell F10 type `=E10`.

13. In cell F11 type `=E11-E10`.

14. In cell F12 type `=E12-E11`.
15. In cell F13 type `=SUM(F10:F12)`.
16. In cell F6 type `=SUM(F10:F13)-E6`.

D	E	F
	Actual	Meter use Only
Cash	$ 2,997,978	$ 5,002,022
	Meter Level	Difference
Red	$ 1,000,000	$ 1,000,000
Yellow	$ 3,000,000	$ 2,000,000
Green	$ 4,000,000	$ 1,000,000
		$ 4,000,000

We will use column E later to set the green, yellow, and red levels for the user. Column **F** will set the difference between those levels to ultimately control the meter. A speedometer chart in Excel is effectively an optical illusion and the **Meter Use Only** field is used to make the illusion work.

Some more formatting

While we're formatting things, let's clean up some of the pivot tables, which we'll be using for drill-down, by adding some headings.

1. Select the **Revenue** worksheet.
2. On the left, select rows 1 and 2; not A1 and A2, the complete row.
3. Right-click and select **Insert**.
4. Type `Revenue`.
5. Hit *Ctrl + B* to make the item bold.

	A	B	C	D	E
1	Revenue				
2					
3	Account Category Number	(Multiple Items) ⟋			
4					
5	Sum of Amount	Column Labels ⟋			
6		⊟ 2017			
7	Row Labels ▾	1	2	3	4
8	000-4100-00	-	-	539.55	8,792.14
9	000-4110-01	3,799.00	-	2,659.30	579.65
10	000-4110-02	55,497.10	24,308.85	172,251.95	220,818.15
11	000-4140-00	-	-	419.40	-
12	Grand Total	59,296.10	24,308.85	175,870.20	230,189.94

Excel offers a number of different options to format data the same way. In this case, to bold an item, we can click the large **B** on the ribbon or press *Ctrl + B*, or right-click and then select **Format Cells | Font | Font Style: Bold,** or expand the **Font** section of the ribbon and hit **Bold**. There are probably a few more ways. The formatting techniques in this book are designed to work consistently, but they aren't necessarily the most efficient. I want to encourage you to find the best way of formatting based on how you work.

6. Select the **Net Income** worksheet.

7. On the left, select rows 1 and 2; not just cells A1 and A2, but the complete row A.

8. Right-click and select **Insert**.

9. Type Net Income.

10. Hit *Ctrl + B* to bold the item.

11. Repeat this process for the **Receivables Aging, Top 10 Customers**, and **Cash** worksheets.

You'll notice that the dashboard items don't break just because we're moving the columns around in the underlying sheets.

I want to wrap up this chapter with some formatting recommendations:

- **Don't go overboard with different fonts and styles**: We're exploring lots of options, but you don't have to use them all in every dashboard. Remember, you're going for understanding. You're not expressing your inner kindergartner.

- **Be careful using currency symbols**: Overusing them makes information hard to read. If data is being displayed in multiple currencies, you'll need to express that, but every data point shouldn't need a dollar or Euro sign. When possible, note the currency above or below the presented data. This is a cluttered currency presentation:

Sum of Amount	Column Labels				2017 Total
	2017				
Row Labels	1	2	3	4	
000-4100-00	$ -	$ -	$ 539.55	$ 8,792.14	$ 9,331.69
000-4110-01	$ 3,799.00	$ -	$ 2,659.30	$ 579.65	$ 7,037.95
000-4110-02	$ 55,497.10	$ 24,308.85	$172,251.95	$ 220,818.15	$ 472,876.05
000-4140-00	$ -	$ -	$ 419.40	$ -	$ 419.40
000-4510-01	$ (29,272.62)	$(12,093.06)	$ (91,227.81)	$ (111,630.94)	$ (244,224.43)
000-4600-00	$ -	$ 1.60	$ 89.90	$ 23.94	$ 115.44
000-5100-00	$ (63,045.68)	$(28,147.81)	$ (29,141.84)	$ (29,019.39)	$ (149,354.72)
100-5150-00	$ (1,431.65)	$ (1,430.24)	$ (1,432.12)	$ (1,431.83)	$ (5,725.84)
100-5170-00	$ (900.00)	$ (393.93)	$ (408.41)	$ (406.60)	$ (2,108.94)
200-5170-00	$ (3,848.23)	$ (1,684.56)	$ (1,746.19)	$ (1,738.60)	$ (9,017.58)
300-5130-00	$ (1,778.92)	$ (729.29)	$ (5,276.16)	$ (6,905.75)	$ (14,690.12)
500-6150-00	$ -	$ -	$ (15.00)	$ -	$ (15.00)
Grand Total	$ (40,981.00)	$ (20,168.44)	$ 46,712.57	$ 79,080.77	$ 64,643.90

Removing the symbols makes it much cleaner:

Net Income					
Posting Type	Profit and Loss		US $		
Sum of Amount	Column Labels				2017 Total
	2017				
Row Labels	1	2	3	4	
000-4100-00	-	-	539.55	8,792.14	9,331.69
000-4110-01	3,799.00	-	2,659.30	579.65	7,037.95
000-4110-02	55,497.10	24,308.85	172,251.95	220,818.15	472,876.05
000-4140-00	-	-	419.40	-	419.40
000-4510-01	(29,272.62)	(12,093.06)	(91,227.81)	(111,630.94)	(244,224.43)
000-4600-00	-	1.60	89.90	23.94	115.44

- **Hide the decimal points**: If your organization is large enough to be using Microsoft Dynamics GP 2013, decimal points don't matter when analyzing financial data. Plus, they clutter up the screen. That's why we took them out of the data presented on the dashboard.

Summary

In this chapter our dashboard is starting to take shape. We built a revenue and expense table and formatted the information with color and icon sets. We built a top ten customers list and highlighted the relative importance of those customers with data bars. We formatted some secondary data with Color Scales, and we used a number of formatting techniques in Microsoft Excel 2013. Best of all, we got two of the five major elements built for our dashboard.

Through the remaining chapters, we will do some additional formatting as we clean things up and bring the whole dashboard together. For now, it's time to add some real sexiness to our dashboard with charts.

5
Charts: Eye Candy for Executives

Charts are eye candy for executives. They make a dashboard look great. Charts can simplify complex data. They can reveal patterns and trends. Charts can also clutter up a dashboard and make it hard to read. There are tons of resources available on the web for building charts in Excel, so we won't dig into every aspect of charting. We will focus on the elements we need for our dashboard. These represent some of the most common charts for dashboards. After the easy stuff, we'll do an uncommon, but really useful speedometer chart. Finally, we'll look at a different type of chart, a **Sparkline**. Specifically, we're going to build the following:

- Combo bar and line chart for revenue and net income
- Pie chart for receivables
- Speedometer chart for cash
- Bar chart with a trend line
- Sparklines

The theme of communication and understanding continues with charts. Charts in a dashboard should be simple and easy to understand. They should make information clearer. Avoid the fancy 3D charts. They tend to be harder to understand. At the end of this chapter, we will look at some resources for selecting the right chart.

Recap

As a reminder, we are working to build a dashboard that looks like this:

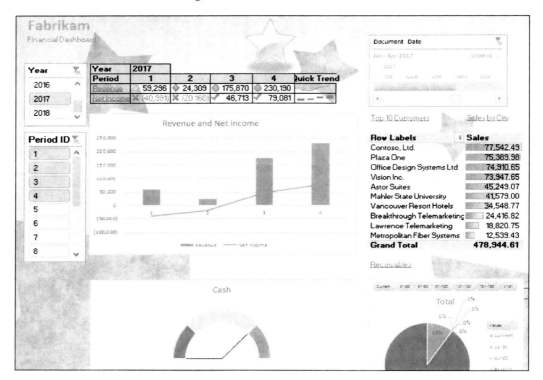

Through the first four chapters we built the framework of our dashboard and started formatting. So far, the main dashboard should look similar to the following:

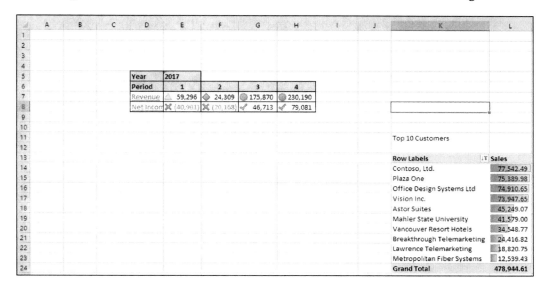

With this chapter, the dashboard really comes together.

 I'm not sure what's going on with the dessert theme in this chapter but we look at bars, pies, and doughnuts. Maybe I was just hungry when I wrote this.

Bar chart

For our dashboard we're going to add a bar chart showing revenue over time to enhance our revenue table. Then we'll layer over a line to show net income as a complement to revenue. With this technique, we can show income, even when it's technically a loss, against revenue.

Let's start building our bar chart. To build a revenue chart:

1. Open the GP 2013 `Dashboard.xlsx` file that we've been working with.
2. Select the **Dashboard** worksheet.

3. Highlight cells D7 through H8. This should be the revenue and net income information from the table.

Year	2017			
Period	1	2	3	4
Revenue	△ 59,296	◇ 24,309	◯ 175,870	◯ 230,190
Net Income	✗ (40,981)	✗ (20,168)	✓ 46,713	✓ 79,081

4. Select the **Insert** tab from the ribbon.
5. Select **Recommended Charts** from the ribbon.
6. Select the first option, **Clustered Column**, and click **OK**.

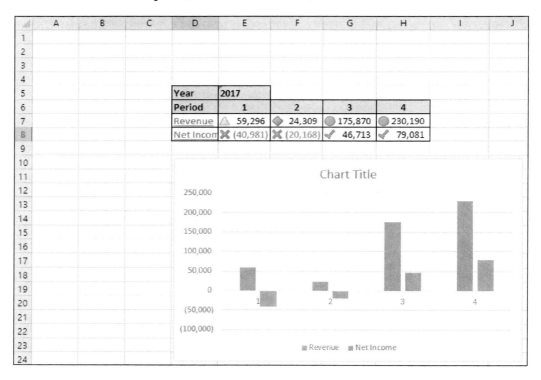

7. Drag the chart to anchor the upper-left corner in cell D10.

Adding a line

Let's see how we can add a line:

1. Right-click on the chart and select **Change Chart Type**.
2. Select **Combo** on the left.
3. Select the first option on the top right, **Clustered Column – Line** and click **OK**.

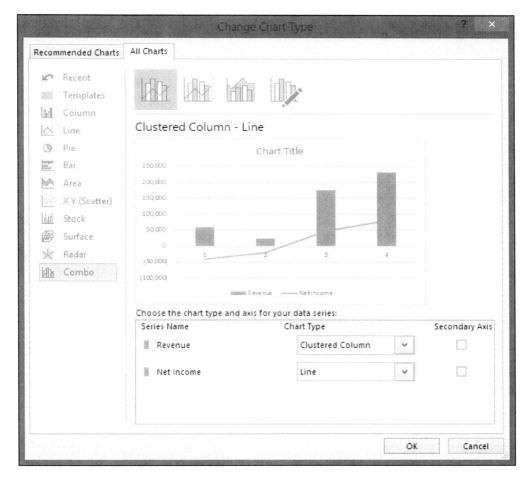

4. Click on the chart title and rename it `Revenue and Net Income`.
5. Save the file.

You'll notice that this combo chart displays negative net income without cluttering up revenue. Now we've got our combo chart for revenue and net income. Next up, let's look at receivables.

Pie chart

Pie charts are useful for showing percentages and portions. They are great for segmenting data. In our dashboard we want to show the breakdown of receivables to understand what buckets our receivables fall into. In other words, what percentage of our receivables are new and what percentages are aged at various lengths.

To build our receivables aging pie chart:

1. Select the **Receivables Aging** worksheet.

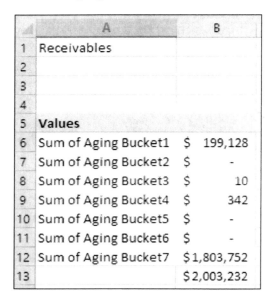

	A	B
1	Receivables	
2		
3		
4		
5	**Values**	
6	Sum of Aging Bucket1	$ 199,128
7	Sum of Aging Bucket2	$ -
8	Sum of Aging Bucket3	$ 10
9	Sum of Aging Bucket4	$ 342
10	Sum of Aging Bucket5	$ -
11	Sum of Aging Bucket6	$ -
12	Sum of Aging Bucket7	$ 1,803,752
13		$ 2,003,232

2. Click in cell A2 to select the pivot table.
3. On the ribbon, select **Insert | Recommended Charts | Pie** and click **OK**.

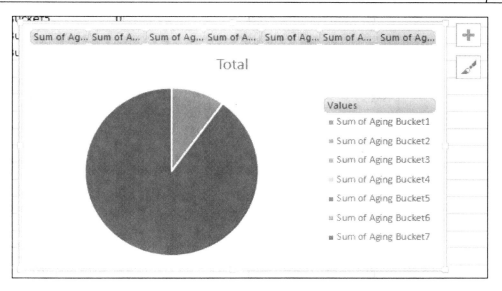

4. Click on the blue pie to select it.
5. Right-click on the pie and select **Add Data Labels | Add Data Labels**.
6. Click on one of the data labels.
7. Right-click and select **Format Data Labels**.
8. In the **Format Data Labels** section on the right, check **Percentage** and uncheck **Value**:

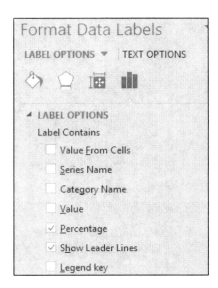

9. In the pivot table, change the value of cell A2 to **Current**.

10. Repeat this process with all the items in column **A** to match this table:

Value
Current
31-60
61-90
91-120
121-150
151-180
>180

The values will change in the chart as well.

11. Select the chart, right-click, and select **Cut**.

12. Select the **Dashboard** worksheet.

13. Select cell K23 on the **Dashboard** worksheet.

14. Right-click and select **Paste**.

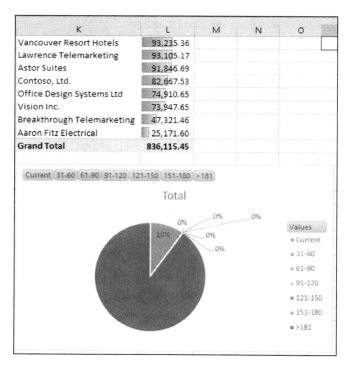

15. Click on the pie chart.

16. Grab the sizing handle on the right and shrink the chart to fit in columns **K** and **L**.

Now we've got a breakout of the receivables aging. This is sample data, but in a real business this looks bad. Ninety percent of our receivables are over 180 days. That's a scary scenario.

 If your company's aging looks like this, yikes! Typically, companies don't have most of their receivables in the longest timeframe. I decided to leave it like this, even though the sample data isn't terribly realistic. I think you are smart enough to understand what this might look like in the real world.

Speedometer chart

A speedometer chart is a classic dashboard presentation tool, but it's not a chart available in Microsoft Excel. Excel guru and Microsoft MVP, Mr Excel, offers a speedometer chart add-in for Excel for $99. But it doesn't work with versions greater than 2003, so we're going to build one.

Speedometer charts are just what you would expect. Like a car speedometer, a speedometer chart has a dial and a needle with the needle moving from left to right depending on the value. They are extremely useful for showing levels. In our case we're going to build one that shows the level of cash. We'll add some red, yellow, and green indicators to help users understand whether the level of cash is acceptable. Our finished speedometer chart should look a lot like this:

Because a speedometer chart doesn't exist as a type in Excel 2013, we are going to build it with an optical illusion. Our speedometer chart uses half of a pie chart to make the needle and half of a doughnut chart to make the dial. With all of these pies and doughnuts, I'm getting hungry!

Building a doughnut

Since this isn't a standard chart, it takes a little more work to build one. We've already laid the foundation in the last chapter, so we're ready to start building. To build a speedometer chart:

1. Continue with the GP 2013 Dashboard.xlsx file that we've been using.
2. Select the **Cash** worksheet.
3. Highlight cells F10 through F13. These should be under the header **Difference**.
4. Click **Insert** to open the insert ribbon.
5. Select the pie chart drop-down in the **Charts** section.
6. Select the **Doughnut** chart.

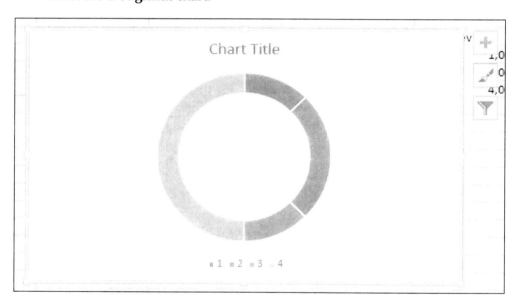

7. Slowly click the largest slice of the doughnut twice to select it. You have to click twice with a little time in between to just select a slice.
8. Right-click on the largest slice and select **Format Data Point**.

9. The **Format Data Point** sidebar opens on the right. Choose the icon that looks like a graph. Change the value of **Angle of First Slice** to 270 and hit *Enter*. This rotates the doughnut to put the total slice on the bottom.

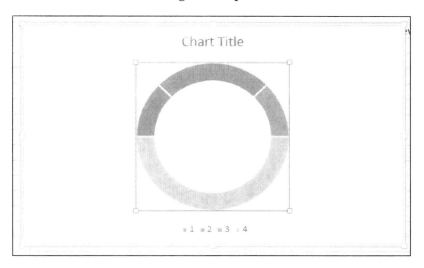

Cutting the doughnut in half

This is how it's done:

1. With the largest segment still selected, select the paint bucket icon in the **Format Data Options** sidebar.
2. Check the box for **No Fill** to make the segment disappear.
3. Select the legend at the bottom of the chart and click the *Delete* key.

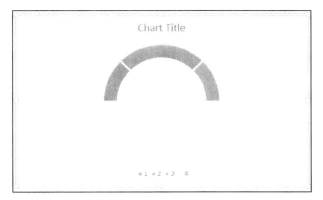

4. Slowly click twice to select the leftmost visible segment.

5. Right-click and select **Format Data Point**.

6. On the **Format Data Point** sidebar, click on the paint bucket icon.

7. Change the color to red.

8. Repeat this process with the middle slice and change the color to yellow.

9. Finally, do this one more time with the rightmost slice and change the color to green.

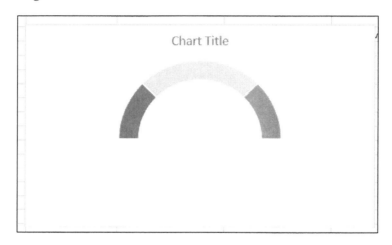

Building a needle

Now we have the outside dial of our speedometer chart. Up next we'll build the needle with a pie chart. To do this:

1. Right-click inside the doughnut chart.

2. Click **Select Data**.

3. Click **Add** to add a second data series.

4. Under **Series Name** type Cash.

5. Clear the **Series Value** box and use your mouse to select cells E6 and F6 and click **OK** twice. These are the values under the **Actual** and **Meter Use Only** headings.

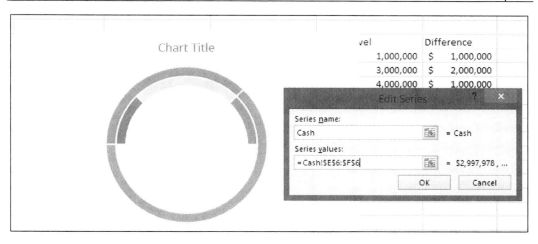

6. Slowly click the largest section of the outer ring twice to select it.
7. Right-click the largest section of the outer ring and select **Format Data Point**.
8. On the **Format Data Point** sidebar to the left, click the icon that resembles a graph.
9. Click on the paint bucket icon and set **Fill** to **None** and **Border** to **None**.

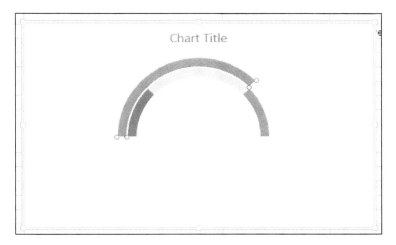

10. Slowly click the remaining visible outer ring section twice to select it.
11. Right-click and select **Change Series Chart Type**.

12. On the bottom, change the drop-down for the **Cash** series from **Doughnut** to **Pie** and click **OK**:

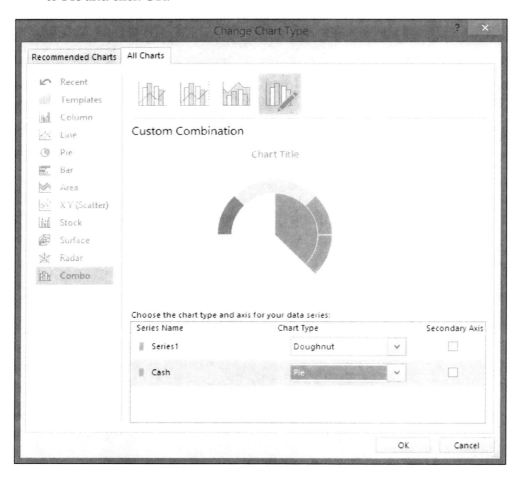

13. Slowly double-click on the filled-in section in the center of the chart to select it.

14. Right-click on the filled-in section in the center of the chart and select **Format Data Point**.

15. Select the icon that resembles a graph and set **Angle of first slice** to 270.

16. Click on the paint bucket icon and set **Fill** to **No Fill**.

17. Set **Border** to **Solid Line**.

18. Set the color of the border to black:

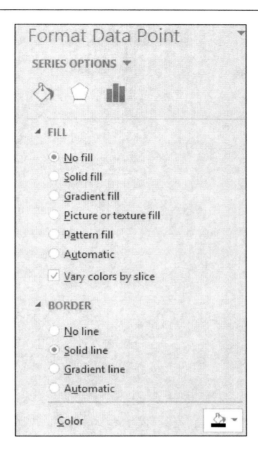

By now you should see the framework of our speedometer chart taking shape. We have red, yellow, and green indicators with a needle showing our position on the scale:

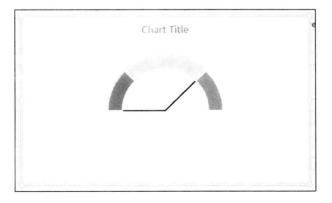

Finishing it off with sprinkles

We need to finish formatting our chart and move it onto our dashboard. To finish things up:

1. Slowly double-click the center needle. You want to select the section in the upper left.

2. Right-click and select **Add Data Label** | **Add Data Label** to display the value of the cash amount.

3. Drag this value down below the meter.

4. Double-click on **Chart Title** and change it to **Cash**.

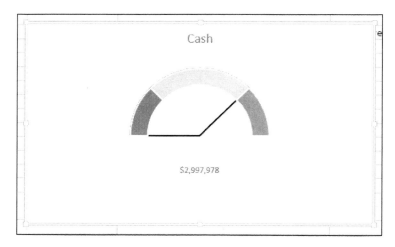

5. Right-click in the white space of the chart to select the whole chart.

6. Click **Cut**.

7. Select the **Dashboard** worksheet.

8. Select cell D27.

9. Right-click and select **Paste** to paste the chart onto the dashboard.

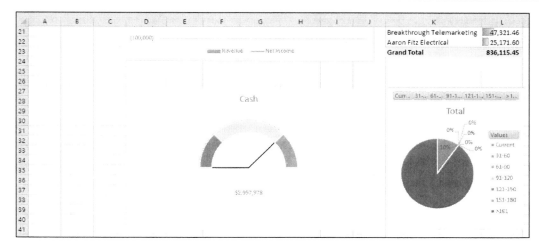

That is how you build a speedometer chart in Excel 2013. It's a lot of steps, but once you understand how it's built, the process is very straightforward.

Ok, so maybe "Finish it off with sprinkles" took the doughnut metaphor too far.

This speedometer chart is loosely based on the technique described at `http://www.brainbell.com/tutorials/ms-office/excel/Create_A_Speedometer_Chart.htm`. (short link: `http://bit.ly/13LssJN`) You can find some additional information there.

Bar chart with trend line

Charts are great for visually displaying trends, but sometimes the actual trend is hard to distinguish. Chart values can vary significantly, making it difficult to determine a true trend. Fortunately, Excel 2013 allows us to add a true, statistically significant trend line to some charts. This type of analysis is also called a **regression analysis**. With Excel 2013 we can even extend the trend to predict values beyond what's in the chart. We won't be using one in this dashboard, but it's useful in many dashboard scenarios for forecasting, so it's worth covering.

To build a trend line into a chart we have to use a particular layout for the chart. Let's set up a chart and add a trend line to it:

1. Select the **Revenue** tab.

2. Highlight the pivot table, right-click, and select **Copy**.

3. Select cell A15, right-click, and select **Paste**.

4. Select the new pivot table. If the pivot table field list doesn't appear on the right, select **Analyze** under the **Pivottable Tools** ribbon area and select **Field List**.

5. In **Field List**, drag **Year** to **Filters**.

6. Drag **Account Number** to **Columns**.

7. Drag **Periods** to **Row Labels**:

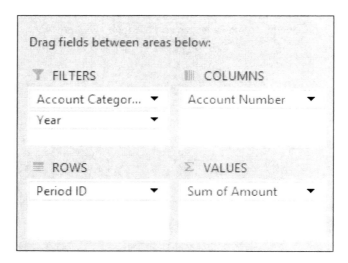

8. Select the amounts on the **Grand Total** row of the pivot table.

9. From the ribbon, select **Insert** | **PivotChart** | **PivotChart**.

10. Select the **Cluster Column** chart and click **OK**.

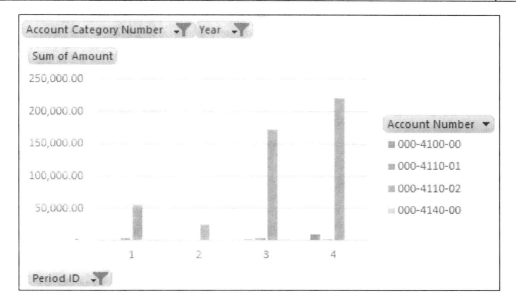

Now we have a chart. We just need to add a trend line. To add a trend line:

1. Right-click on the largest bar on the chart. All the tall bars should get selected.

2. Click on **Add Trendline**.

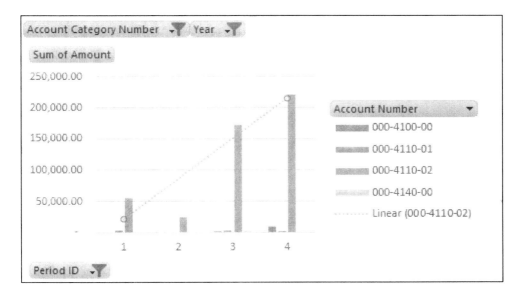

By default, Excel 2013 creates a linear trend line, but we're not limited to that. We can change the statistical rationale behind our trend line with the **Format Trendline** sidebar on the right. For example:

1. Select the box next to **Logarithmic** to set a trend that tapers off over time.

2. In the **Forecast** section at the bottom, change the value of **Forward** to 2 to see the expected revenue growth over the next two periods:

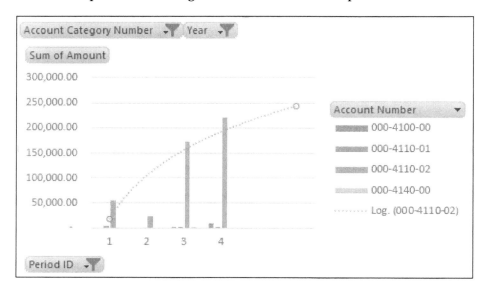

3. Drag the chart to an empty spot to the right of the new pivot table.

4. Save the file.

It helps to have some understanding of statistics to pick the best trend line, but here is some basic guidance:

Linear	This is a best-fit line ideally used with simple data sets where the data points resemble a straight line. Usually this shows an increase or decrease at a steady state.
Logarithmic	This is a best-fit curved line when the rate of change increases or decreases and then levels out.
Polynomial	A polynomial line is a curved line that is used when data fluctuates. It can be useful with large data sets.
Power	Curved line used to compare data that increases at a specified rate.

| **Exponential** | Used when data values rise or fall at constantly increasing rates. |
| **Moving Average** | Smoothes fluctuations in data to show a pattern or trend more clearly. |

 For more information on trend lines and the statistics behind them, Microsoft offers some help at `http://office.microsoft.com/en-us/excel-help/add-change-or-remove-a-trendline-in-a-chart-HP010007461.aspx`. (short link: `http://bit.ly/ZxIoJC`)

Selecting charts

One of the problems that users often have with charts is choosing which chart to use for different types of data. To help users select the right chart, visual business intelligence company **Perceptual Edge** has created a one-page tool to help users select the right data. It can be downloaded from: `http://www.perceptualedge.com/articles/misc/Graph_Selection_Matrix.pdf`. This is how it looks:

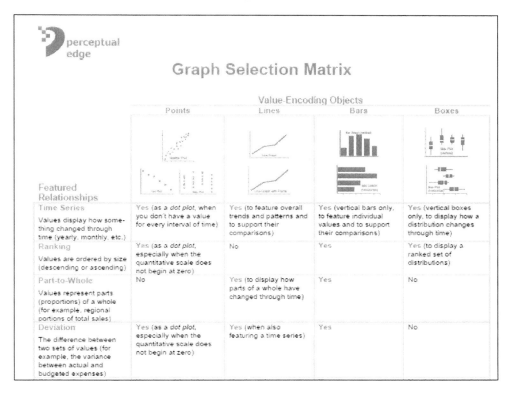

Sparklines

Sparklines provide a way to show a quick trend on data. Unlike traditional Excel charts, sparklines fit in a single cell and are designed to show things such as a quick trend for a subset of information.

Preparing for sparklines

Sparklines are mini-charts placed in an individual cell and designed to display information from a single row of cells. They are a great way to provide a quick snapshot of key data. We'll add some sparklines to our revenue and net income data. First let's set up the formatting:

1. Open the GP 2013 `Dashboard.xlsx` file that we've been working with.
2. Click the **Dashboard** tab to open the worksheet.
3. Select cell I6. This should be the cell next to the header for period **4**.
4. Type `Quick Trend` in cell I6 and widen the cell to ensure that it fits.
5. Select cell H6.
6. Select the **Home** tab and click the paintbrush icon to copy the formatting.
7. Click on cell I6 to apply the formatting.

Year	2017				
Period	1	2	3	4	Quick Trend
Revenue	△ 59,296	◇ 24,309	◉ 175,870	◉ 230,190	
Net Income	✗ (40,981)	✗ (20,168)	✓ 46,713	✓ 79,081	

Adding sparklines

Now that we're set up, let's build a sparkline:

1. Highlight cells E7 through H7. These are the amounts on the **Revenue** line.
2. Click **Insert** to open the insert ribbon.
3. In the **Sparklines** section, click **Line**.
4. The **Create Sparklines** box will open. The **Data Range** box will be pre-populated with the highlighted cells.

5. Select the **Location** box and click on the lookup button next to it.

6. Pick cell I7 and hit *Enter.*

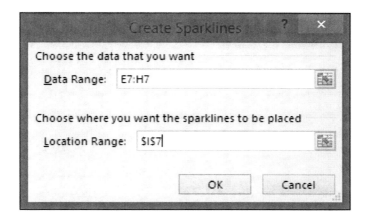

7. Click **OK** to create the sparkline.

Year	2017				
Period	1	2	3	4	Quick Trend
Revenue	△ 59,296	◇ 24,309	● 175,870	● 230,190	
Net Income	✖ (40,981)	✖ (20,168)	✔ 46,713	✔ 79,081	

Adding a sparkline to cell I7 creates a small line graph in that cell. It's a great way to get a quick read on how the data has moved. Let's add another sparkline to the net income line. This time we'll add a column chart and adjust the view to show negatives.

To add a sparkline to the **Net Income** row as shown in the screenshot:

1. Highlight cells E8 through H8.

2. Click **Insert** to open the insert ribbon.

3. In the **Sparklines** section, click **Line**.

4. The **Create Sparklines** box will open. The **Data Range** box will be pre-populated with the highlighted cells.

5. Select the **Location** box and click on the lookup button next to it.

6. Select cell I8 and hit *Enter*.

7. Click **OK** to create the sparkline.

Year	2017				
Period	1	2	3	4	Quick Trend
Revenue	△ 59,296	◆ 24,309	⬤ 175,870	⬤ 230,190	
Net Income	✖ (40,981)	✖ (20,168)	✔ 46,713	✔ 79,081	

8. Select the sparkline in cell I8.

9. The tab for the **Sparkline Tools Design** ribbon lights up.

10. Select the **Sparkline Tools Design** ribbon.

11. Check the **Negative Points** box in the **Show** section.

12. On the column sparkline, the first two data points will turn red to indicate that these are negative numbers:

Year	2017				
Period	1	2	3	4	Quick Trend
Revenue	△ 59,296	◆ 24,309	⬤ 175,870	⬤ 230,190	
Net Income	✖ (40,981)	✖ (20,168)	✔ 46,713	✔ 79,081	

13. Select cells I7 and I8 to finish formatting the cells.

14. Right-click and select **Format Cells**.

15. Pick the **Border** tab.

16. Click the **Outline** and **Inside** boxes to put lines around the sparkline cells.

17. Click **OK** to finish.

18. Save the file.

The **Sparkline Tools Design** tab lights up when you select a sparkline. It contains additional tools to improve the usability of sparklines. For example:

- Selecting **Sparkline Tools Design | Edit Data | Hidden and Empty Cells** will allow you to control blank data points. You can show a gap in your sparkline, default that point to zero, or simply connect lines skipping the gap.

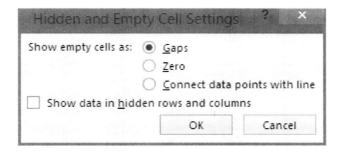

- With the options in the **Show** section you can mark data points such as the high and low points, first and last points, and negative numbers.

Sparkline idiosyncrasies

Sparklines are an interesting combination of charts and cells. This combination creates some idiosyncrasies when working with them. As we wrap up sparklines we'll look at a few.

Deleting sparklines

Since sparklines reside in a cell, you might think that you can simply hit the *Delete* button and remove a sparkline, but you can't. To remove a sparkline, select the sparkline, right-click, and select **Sparklines | Clear Selected Sparklines**.

Changing sparkline data

Sparklines are attached to a selection of cells in a row. In our case, we don't have them directly connected to a pivot table. Our revenue and income boxes are intentionally not dynamic, so putting a sparkline to the right works. If we connect a sparkline to a pivot table row, changes to the pivot table can cause it to grow beyond the location of the sparkline. The pivot table overlaps the sparkline and the sparkline appears behind the overlapping data. Usually, this isn't ideal. If you're connecting a sparkline directly to a pivot table, consider adding it to the left or farther out to the right.

Since sparklines are based on a range, adding data to a cell outside the range will not be picked up by a sparkline. For example, if sparkline data runs from cells E7 to H7, adding data in D7 will not change the sparkline. Adding a cell in the middle of the range will update a sparkline. Named ranges can be used when creating a sparkline to help overcome this limitation.

Like any other cell, sparklines can be cut, copied, and pasted to a different cell. The cells they are in can be formatted with backgrounds and borders.

Summary

With this chapter we've made huge progress on our dashboard. You should see it taking shape in front of you. The charts add significant visual elements to the pivot tables we added previously. Sparklines provide a way to add small chart elements within a pivot table. They are great for getting a quick feel for where the data has been going.

But a dashboard without interactivity is still just a fancy report. We need to give users a controlled ability to make changes and explore. We want to give end users the right to change dates or departments so that we don't have to do that for them. We want to let users explore the data safely. The key to that is slicers.

In the next chapter, we will add interactivity to our dashboard with slicers and a new kind of date-based slicer—a Timeline.

6

Adding Interactivity with Slicers and Timelines

We've made a lot of progress with our dashboard, but we've still got some elements to go. In this chapter, we'll wrap up the core pieces of the dashboard with a look at slicers, including a new type of slicer, the timeline.

A dashboard without interactivity is simply a pretty report. Giving users the ability to review scenarios and explore the data is an important part of any dashboard. But you also want to provide enough control over user interaction to ensure that the results are meaningful. For example, if a user selects a year, it's important that all of the related pivot tables update to that year, otherwise a user might be looking at inconsistent data. In this chapter, we will look at elements designed to help provide that interactivity.

Slicers provide a way to give the user additional control over the information being delivered. Excel 2013 added a new type of slicer, the timeline. A timeline is a date-based slicer designed to make it easy for users to work with dates.

In this chapter, we will look at how to create and use:

- Slicers
- Timelines

Recap

As a reminder, we are working to build a dashboard that looks like the following screenshot:

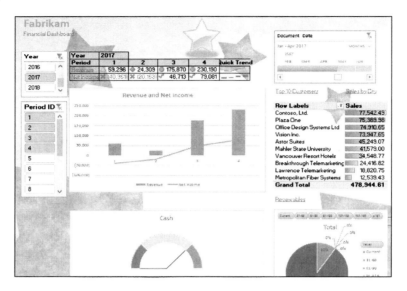

Through the first five chapters we've seen our dashboard come to life with pivot tables, formatting, and charts. This far in, our dashboard should look similar to the following screenshot:

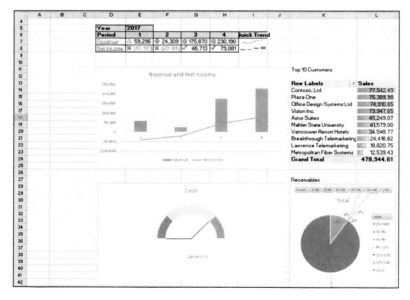

Learning about slicers

Slicers provide interactivity to pivot tables. The simplest definition is that they are replacements for pivot table filters, but that doesn't do them justice. Slicers don't have to be tied to filters, and a slicer can be applied without creating a filter. The key is that slicers are generally easier to use than filters for end users. Some examples of this include:

- When multiple filters are applied at the same level (such as the **Year** and **Period** column filters on our **Revenue** pivot), it can be confusing to the user to select the right level to change the filter.
- Slicers follow the familiar pattern of using the *Shift* key to select all items in a range and the *Ctrl* key to select non-sequential items.
- Slicers can be shared across multiple pivot tables, so one change by the user can affect data in several tables. Filters don't work this way.
- Slicers provide greater formatting options, making it easier to build a good-looking dashboard. They can also be formatted with an Excel theme to match the color of the rest of a workbook.

Creating slicers

Slicers are easy to build, so let's add some slicers to our dashboard to see how powerful they can be. To do this:

1. Select the **Revenue** worksheet in the `Dashboard.xlsx` workbook of GP 2013 that we've been working with.
2. Place the cursor in cell **A5** to select the pivot table.
3. Select the **Insert** ribbon and then click **Slicer**.
4. Check the box next to **Year** to create a slicer based on years.

5. Select the slicer and hit *Ctrl + X* to cut the slicer so we can move it to the dashboard.

6. Move to the dashboard worksheet and select cell B5.

7. Hit *Ctrl + V* to paste the slicer.

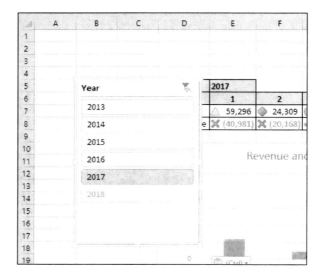

8. Use the handles on the side of the slicer to resize the **Year** slicer to fit roughly into cells B5 through C10. The slicer should show 3 years and a vertical scroll bar.

9. Use the vertical scroll bar to scroll down until the years **2016**, **2017**, and **2018** are being shown in the slicer.

10. Ensure that the year **2017** is selected in the slicer.

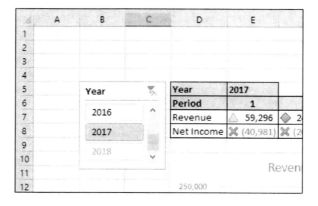

Notice that the year **2018** is greyed out. This is an indicator that there is no data for 2018 that matches either our slicers or filters. There may be 2018 data, but there isn't any for 2018 for period **1** to **4** and the filtered accounts that we are using. Remember that we've already pre-filtered our pivot table, and the slicer is acting on that pivot table.

Now that we've sliced on years, let's go ahead and slice on periods as well. To add a period slicer:

1. Select the **Revenue** worksheet in the `Dashboard.xlsx` workbook of GP 2013 that we've been working with.

2. Place the cursor in cell A5 to select the pivot table.

3. Select the **Insert** ribbon and then click on **Slicer**.

4. Check the box next to **Period ID** to create a slicer based on periods.

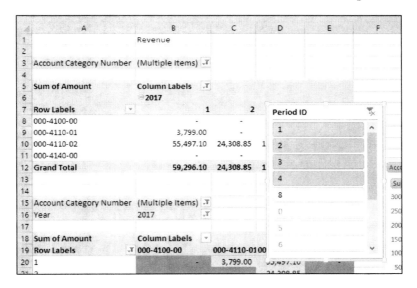

5. Select the slicer and hit *Ctrl + X* to cut the slicer so we can move it to the dashboard.

6. Move to the dashboard worksheet and select cell **B12**.

7. Hit *Ctrl + V* to paste the slicer.

8. Use the handles on the side of the slicer to resize the **Period** slicer to fit roughly into cells **B12** through **C24**.

9. Hold down the *Ctrl* button and select periods **1** through **4** in the **Period** slicer.

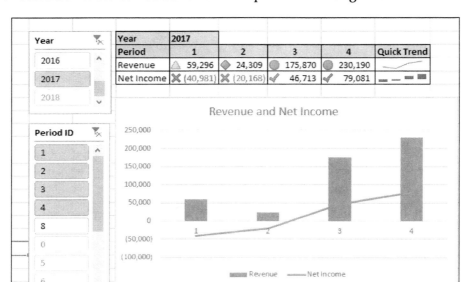

In the **Period ID** slicer, select just period **1** and watch the graph move. Repeat this with period **2**. Notice the animation of the bars as the graph changes. This is a new Excel 2013 feature. Animating charts used to be really hard to do, but Excel 2013 makes it easy.

Let's dig a little deeper into our slicers for just a minute:

In the **Period ID** slicer, hold down *Ctrl* and select period **1, 2, 3**, and **8**.

Notice that in our table, **Net Income** shows a **#REF** error. This is because our slicer is really only connected to our **Revenue** pivot table. Because the GETPIVOTDATA formulas look at the table headers, the **Net Income** graph moves around, but it's really not being driven by the slicer.

Connecting slicers

Slicers can be connected to a single set of data, or they can be shared. If we want revenue and net income reporting to move together, and we usually do, we can connect a single slicer to both sets of data. This is much more convenient to the user than having to change the settings on slicers for each dataset. If we were only using filters, the user would have to change the filters for revenue and net income. To connect our slicers to net income as well as revenue:

1. Right-click on the **Year** slicer and select **Report Connections**.
2. Check the box next to **Net Income** and click on **OK**.

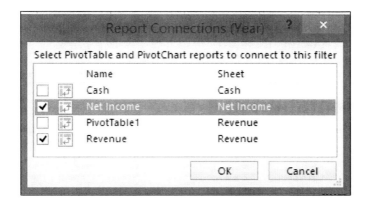

3. Back on the **Dashboard** tab, right-click on the **Period ID** slicer and select **Report Connections**.
4. Check the box next to **Net Income** and click on **OK**.

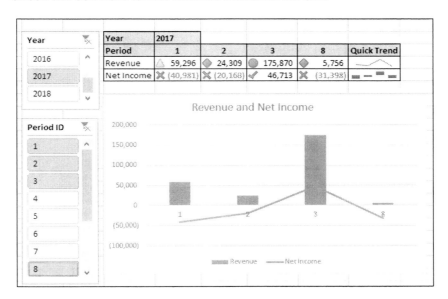

Once you connect the **Period ID** slicer, the net income error in period **8** disappears, and the graph rebuilds with the appropriate information.

5. On the **Period ID** slicer, hold the **Shift** button and select periods **1** and **4** to select the range.

6. We normally want to see revenue and income for the same periods. It doesn't make much sense to evaluate revenue from January against net income from August. Connecting these two pivot tables with a single slicer not only makes things easier for the user, it helps keep them out of trouble too.

Slicer orientation

The two slicers that we've created so far are vertical slicers, that is, the selections are oriented up and down. Depending on how a dashboard is laid out, it may make sense to orient some slicers horizontally. We won't use one in this dashboard, but we will create a quick example, so you can see how to do it. To create a horizontal slicer:

1. Select the **Year** slicer on the **Dashboard** worksheet.

2. Press *Ctrl + C* to copy the slicer.

3. Press *Ctrl + V* to paste in the copy.

4. Drag the copied **Year** slicer to cell **F2**.

5. Right-click on the copied slicer and select **Slicer Properties**.

6. Change the **Caption** in **Slicer Properties** to **Year (Horizontal)**, so that we can differentiate the 2-year slicers.

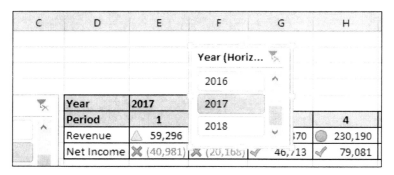

7. Click on the **Year (Horizontal)** slicer. On the ribbon, a new tab lights up, **Slicer Tools Options**.

8. Click on the **Slicer Tools Options** tab.

9. Change the **Columns** field to 4 to set the number of columns across.

10. Click on the **Year (Horizontal)** slicer again.

11. Use the handles to resize the slicer to fit in cells **F2** to **I5**.

12. Adjust the size to only show one row of years.

D	E	F	G	H	I
		Year (Horizontal)			
		2013	2014	2015	2016
Year	2017				
Period	1	2	3	4	Quick Trend
Revenue	△ 59,296	◇ 24,309	◯ 175,870	◯ 230,190	
Net Income	✗ (40,981)	✗ (20,168)	✓ 46,713	✓ 79,081	

Now we have a long, narrow slicer that can be a great fit for the top of a pivot table. Since we're going to delete this slicer before we're done, let's play with a few more settings.

Slicer options

Let's explore some of the other things that we can do to format slicers. First, we can control how slicers behave with respect to cells. To do so, follow these steps:

1. Right-click on the **Year (Horizontal)** slicer and pick **Size and Properties**.

2. Scroll down to the **Properties** section and expand it with the arrow next to **Properties** if necessary.

The **Properties** section lets you control how the slice moves with respect to cells. The options are:

Option	Function
Move and size with cells	Slicer moves with cells (move, sort, and so on) and gets wider, narrow, taller, or shorter as cells are resized.
Move but don't size with cells	Slicer moves with cells (move, sort, and so on) but changes to cell sizes don't affect the slicer.
Don't move or size with cells	Changes to cells don't reposition the slicer.

If the **Print object** box is checked in the **PROPERTIES** section, the slicers will print when the workbook is printed. If it's unchecked, the slicers won't print. Also located on this window, in the **POSITION AND LAYOUT** section, is a **Disable resizing and moving** checkbox. Checking this box will prevent users from repositioning or resizing the slicers. Consider checking this box when you are done with your dashboard to keep users from accidently dragging slicers around. Refer to the following screenshot:

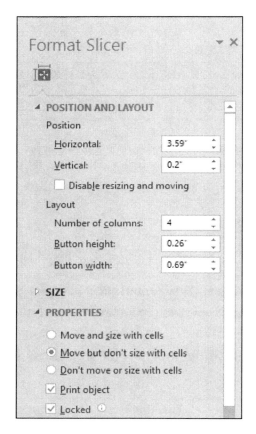

Additional options are available by right-clicking on a slicer and selecting **Slicer Options**. From this window, you can:

- Change the internal name of the slicer
- Choose to show or hide the slicer caption. In our example, you could turn on or off the display of **Year (Horizontal)**
- Change the slicer caption that is displayed

- Sort the values on the slicer alphabetically in ascending or descending order

  ° These options are pretty straightforward, but the really interesting options are on the right-hand side. These include:

  ° **Hide items with no data**: If this setting is checked, data that is not available doesn't even show in the slicer. In a previous example, we saw that 2018 was grayed out. If this box was checked, 2018 wouldn't appear in the slicer at all.

  ° **Visually indicate items with no data**: If items without data are not hidden, you can choose to gray them out. This checkbox controls that setting. Checking the box will gray out unavailable options.

  ° **Show items with no data last**: If you choose to gray out unavailable items, you can also choose to automatically move them to the bottom of the list. Sometimes, this produces awkward results. For example, if your list is periods 1 through 12 and periods 4 and 6 have no data, the selection will appear as **1,2,3,5,7,8,9,10,11,12,4,6**. This is confusing the first time users see it. If the list is unordered anyway, this setting makes more sense.

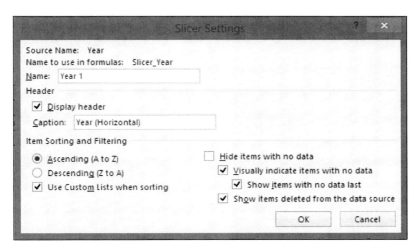

Let's get rid of the **Year (Horizontal)** slicer that we've been playing with. To do this:

1. Select the **Year (Horizontal)** slicer.
2. Press the *Delete* button on the keyboard.

One last point about regular slicers in Excel 2013 is that the slicer doesn't have to be based off data that's visible in the pivot table. For example, we can create a slicer based off of the **Account Description** field even though that field isn't used in the pivot table. To see how to do this:

1. Select the **Revenue** tab.
2. Click in cell **A5** to select the **Revenue** pivot table.
3. Select **Insert | Slicer** from the ribbon.
4. Check the box next to **Account Description** and click on **OK**.

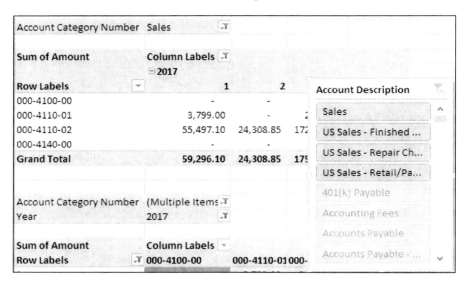

Now we have a slicer based on data that doesn't appear in the pivot table.

 If you check more than one item on the **Insert Slicers** box, Excel will create multiple slicers, one for each checkbox.

5. Click on the **Account Description** slicer and press *Delete*.

Slicers are a great choice for giving dashboard users flexibility without sacrificing complete control. They make it easy for users to change settings while helping them to keep within the framework that you've designed.

With Excel 2013, Microsoft has added a new type of slicer specifically designed for managing date ranges. It's called a timeline. Let's see how we can incorporate a timeline into our dashboard.

Timeline

A timeline is special kind of slicer that is new in Excel 2013. It's designed to work with a range of dates, and it's perfect for working with our **Top 10 Customers** pivot table. Our **Top 10 Customers** pivot table is based around sales over a period of time, so if we want to see the top ten customers based on sales over the last month, quarter, or year, it's easy to adjust the timeline slicer to show that information. The conditional formatting that we've put in place will follow along as well.

Let's add a timeline to our dashboard for the **Top 10 Customers** pivot table. To add this:

1. Select the **Dashboard** tab.
2. Click on cell **K13** to select the **Top 10 Customers** pivot table on the dashboard.
3. Select **Insert | Timeline** to start creating the timeline slicer.
4. On the **Insert Timelines** window, check the box next to **Document Date**.

 Notice that only **Document Date** is available. Timelines only work with dates, so the only fields that are visible in the **Insert Timelines** window are date fields in the pivot table.

5. Click on **OK** to finish creating the timeline slicer.

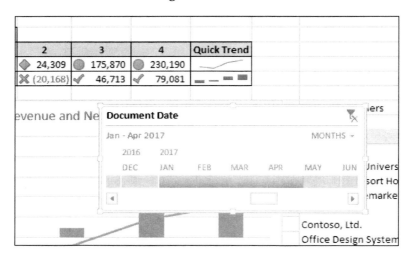

Now that we have our timeline slicer, we need to position it on the page.

6. Drag the timeline so that the upper-left corner rests in cell **K2**.

7. Use the handles to resize the timeline to fit in cells **K2** through **L9**.

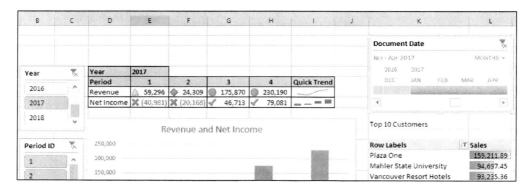

Now we have our timeline to control our **Top 10 Customers** pivot table. Let's see how this works.

1. On the timeline, click **JAN under 2017**. The top 10 customers will be updated to reflect only sales for January.

Notice that **Vancouver Resort Hotels** is the top-selling customer.

2. Hover over the timeline until handles appear to the right-hand side of
   January. Drag the timeline to include **January** through **April** of **2017**. The
   timeline updates to reflect sales for the 4-month period.

With this change, notice that **Contoso, Ltd.** moves to the top of the list. **Vancouver Resorts** moves to the number seven slot. Apparently, Vancouver spent a lot in January and then tapered off. With the change, our list is re-sorted to move the customer with higher sales to the top, and our conditional formatting in the form of data bars is maintained.

The timeline has a horizontal scroll bar at the bottom to move back and forth through the available date range. Above the horizontal line is an indicator to show where you are on the timeline in relation to the selected dates.

 Notice that our slicer field, **Document Date**, doesn't appear at all in the pivot table. The field used in the slicer timeline doesn't have to show in the timeline to still be used to limit the date.

There is a key element to timelines that I don't want you to miss. We did not do anything with the date information to separate it out into months. Excel 2013 did that all by itself. We picked **Document Date** that includes month, day, and year elements, and the timeline defaulted to months. Excel calls this the time level.

What's nice about time level is that we're not limited to whatever Excel 2013 chooses. In our example, next to the word **Months**, is a drop-down box. The drop-down selection contains **Years**, **Quarters**, **Months** and **Days**. Because this is important, let's take a quick look at how this works before we move on:

1. In the **Document Date** timeline, select the drop-down next to the word **Months** and pick **Quarters**. The display will change to reflect **Q1** through **Q4** for each year.

2. Now change **Quarters** to **Days**. The timeline will update to allow you to pick individual days.

3. Finally, set **Days** back to **Months**, since that is most appropriate for our dashboard.

Timeline options

Like traditional slicers, timelines have options to control specific elements of the slicer. We'll take a quick look at the timeline options. To see these options:

1. Select the **Document Date** timeline slicer.

2. A new ribbon lights up named **Timeline Tools Options**.

3. Select the **Timeline Tools Options** ribbon.

We'll walk through the options on the ribbon and dig deeper into some of them:

- The **Timeline Caption** field holds the title that appears at the top of a timeline:

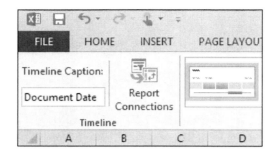

- **Reports Options** work like regular slicers allowing you to connect the timeline to multiple pivot tables:

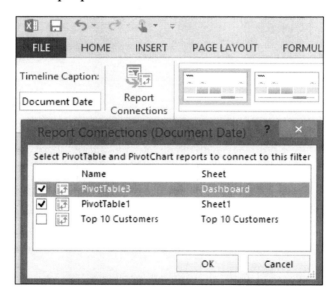

- The **Styles** section in the center makes it easy to change the look and feel of a timeline. This option is available for regular slicers too, as shown in the following screenshot:

On the far right are four key checkboxes for timelines. Let's look at each of them:

- First up, let's have a look at the **Header** element. This controls whether or not the caption is displayed:

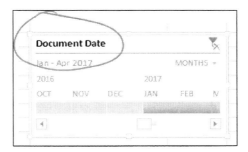

- Next is the **Section Label** element. This displays the period selected in words. In our example, it shows as **Jan - Apr 2017**:

- Up next is the **Scrollbar** element; as mentioned earlier that there is a scroll bar and indicator at the bottom, this shows where you are with respect to the selected time period. This checkbox turns this feature on and off:

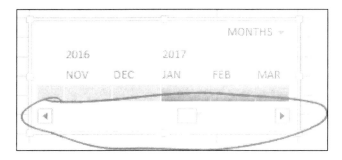

- Finally, we can remove the **Time Level** element:

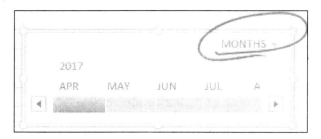

Removing all of these elements results in a timeline with a very small visual footprint. It makes it possible to stuff interactivity into a smaller space, possibly making room for more information on a dashboard.

Consider carefully, though, before removing these items. Elements such as **Header**, **Scrollbar**, and **Section Label** provide important visual cues to users. **Time Level** may allow users to get insights that they wouldn't find otherwise.

So why didn't we use a timeline with revenue and net income? The source data for revenue and net income was not in a date format, that table held a year and a period as separate columns.

Currently, timelines use year, quarter, and month based on a calendar year. I haven't yet found a way to make these respect the fiscal periods that can be used inside of Microsoft Dynamics GP 2013. If you need to use fiscal period instead of calendar periods, you won't be able to effectively use a timeline for now.

There is one element that works for slicers but doesn't work for timelines. That item is disabling, resizing, and moving. To see this:

1. Right-click on our timeline and select **Size and Properties**.

2. On the **Format Timeline** sidebar, expand the **Properties** section. The option to **Disable resizing and moving** is there, but it's grayed out. This is one more consideration when working with timelines.

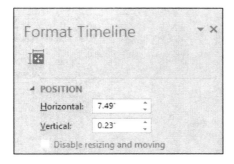

We now have all the core elements of our dashboard built and placed on the **Dashboard** tab. We still have plenty of formatting and cleanup to go, but most of the dashboard is complete.

You may notice that we didn't use slicers on the Cash or open AR sections of the dashboard. This was intentional. Both of these elements are most important for their current value. Knowing my cash position last Thursday doesn't allow me to spend any more or less cash today. The current cash position is the key.

Back to our automobile dashboard example, I need to know my fuel position when driving. It doesn't matter what it was 2 days ago, if I have half a tank, that's all there is. Based on that I can make a decision about whether I need to fill up or not. That's why we put red, yellow, and green indicators around the cash position so that we can tell at a glance whether we need to take action. It may be that when cash falls into the yellow, we need to consider drawing from our credit line. Whatever the action, we know that we need to take action.

Summary

We now have all the key elements of our dashboard on the **Dashboard** tab. There is one more level of interactivity that we will explore in *Chapter 7, Drilling Back to Source Data in Dynamics GP 2013* that includes linking and drilling. Links such as hyperlinks allow you to connect different elements of the dashboard together. Drill backs allow you drill from data in the dashboard back to detailed information in Dynamics GP 2013. Let's connect all the pieces together before we wrap everything up.

7
Drilling Back to Source Data in Dynamics GP 2013

Once you deploy a dashboard, it's inevitable that someone will want more information. They won't believe a number and will want to know the detail that makes up a balance. A great way to manage this is to build a couple of dashboards. Usually, this looks like a primary dashboard with secondary dashboards that break out more information about sales, cash, or departments. We've done this on a very simple level with our Revenue and Net Income tabs. They provide additional detail to expand on the main dashboard numbers.

Another great way to deal with the need for detail, and to take your dashboard beyond what everyone else is doing, is to allow users to drill down into specific transactions or accounts in Microsoft Dynamics GP 2013. In this chapter, we will look at drill down options including:

- Hyperlinks
- Using drill downs present in GP 2013
- The structure of a drill down
- Building your own links with Drill Down Builder
- Drill downs in complex environments

Recap

Throughout the book we've been building a dashboard that looks like the following screenshot:

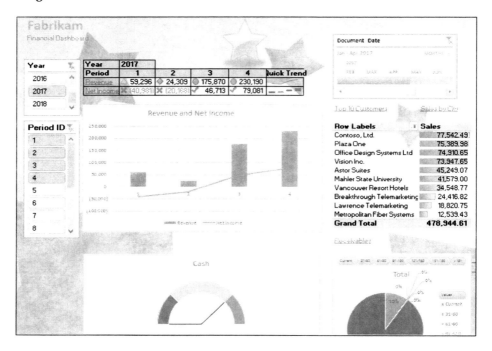

We're done with the hard parts, and now we're connecting the pieces and cleaning things up.

Learning about hyperlinks

Hyperlinks are a feature of Excel 2013 that have been in the product for a while. Links can be built via the interface or with a formula. They provide a great way to link sheets together for the user.

In the previous chapters, we added additional information to our **Revenue** and **Net Income** tabs. We'll start by linking these tabs to our dashboard. To build our hyperlinks:

1. Open the `Dashboard.xlsx` file of GP 2013 that we've been working with.

2. On the **Dashboard** tab, select cell D7. This should be the **Revenue** label.

3. Click on **Insert | Hyperlink** on the Excel ribbon.

4. In the **Link to:** section, on the left-hand side, select **Place in This Document**.

5. In the center section, under **Or select a place in this document:**, pick **Revenue**, as shown in the following screenshot:

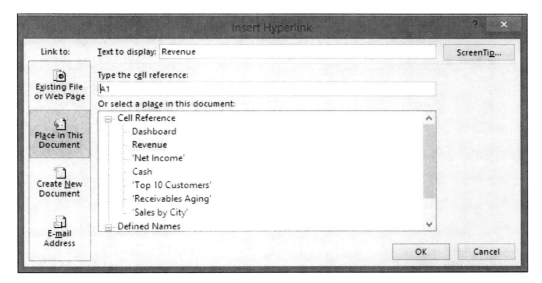

6. Click on **OK**. The **Revenue** label will turn blue and be underlined indicating a hyperlink, as shown in the following screenshot:

Year	2017				
Period	**1**	**2**	**3**	**4**	**Quick Trend**
Revenue	△ 59,296	◇ 24,309	⬤ 175,870	⬤ 230,190	～
Net Income	✗ (40,981)	✗ (20,168)	✓ 46,713	✓ 79,081	▬ ▬ ▬ ▬

7. Click the new **Revenue** link to drill down to the **Revenue** tab.

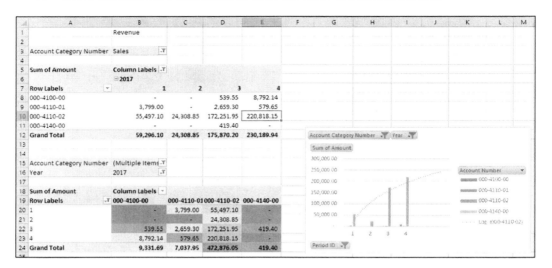

We need to do the same thing for the net Income line. To link to additional net income information, follow these steps:

1. Click on the **Dashboard** tab.
2. On the **Dashboard** tab, select cell E7. This should be the **Net Income** label.
3. Click on **Insert | Hyperlink** on the Excel ribbon.
4. In the **Link to:** section, on the left-hand side, select **Place in This Document**.
5. In the center section under **Or select a place in this Document**, pick '**Net Income**' and click on **OK**.
6. Save the file.
7. Hyperlinks don't have to link back to another Excel sheet. They can also link to more information on the Web or to a location in SharePoint, for example. Finally, we can link them back to a transaction in Dynamics GP 2013. That's up next.

Using drill downs in GP 2013

At its simplest, a drill down is a hyperlink that links back into Dynamics GP. When the user clicks the hyperlink, the focus changes to Microsoft Dynamics GP 2013, and the linked window opens in GP with the appropriate data. In the real world, a dashboard might display cash balances for each bank account, or checkbook in GP terms. The operating checkbook would have a hyperlink attached on the dashboard. Clicking on the link would cause the checkbook register inquiry window to open in Dynamics GP and display information from the operating checkbook.

Drill down background

There are limited training resources available around drill downs. Drill Down Builder gets only a few pages in the SmartList Builder User Guide. Other books on the market that cover SmartList Builder skip Drill Down Builder altogether. When I pushed Microsoft for a list of pre-built drill downs, it couldn't supply one. Also, Microsoft inconsistently uses the terms drill down and drillback interchangeably. For our purposes, they are the same thing.

A drill down link can work for inquiries and transactions throughout GP. Since these drill downs are both poorly documented and numerous, you would think that they would be hard to use, except that Microsoft gave us a huge shortcut. The Office Data Connector files that we've been using for our dashboard contain drill down links. Each ODC file has one or more columns that link back into Dynamics GP. If you can't find the link you are looking for, you can even build your own with the optional Drill Down Builder module from Microsoft.

In this chapter, we're going to build some links, explain how they work, and add some to the dashboard.

Before we get rolling, there are few things that you need to know:

- The user must have Dynamics GP 2013 open and be logged in to the company they are drilling into for the drill down to work. The hyperlink will not open Dynamics GP 2013 for you. This arrangement also makes licensing and security straightforward, since it's controlled by the GP 2013 interface.

- The user must have permission in Dynamics GP 2013 to open the window that they are trying to drill back into. For example, if a user doesn't have access to payroll inquiry via GP, we certainly don't want them to be able to drill down into that data via Excel.

- Drill Down Builder is not required to drill down into Dynamics GP 2013. Drill Down Builder is a part of the optional SmartList Builder product available from Microsoft at an additional cost. Drill Down Builder is used to create drill downs and is covered later in the chapter.

- It is possible to drill down from a local instance of Excel to Microsoft Dynamics GP 2013 on a Citrix server. I didn't say it was easy, but it can be done. We'll look at options at the end of the chapter.

- At the release of Microsoft Dynamics GP 2013, drilling down from Excel to GP via the new web client was not available. It may be made available later via a service pack.

Now that we have all the background out of the way, let's drill down!

Using drill downs

Drill downs are simplest to explain when we bring the data into Microsoft Excel 2013, so we'll go down that route with a common example. To build your first drill down, follow these steps:

1. Open the sample company in Microsoft Dynamics GP 2013.
2. Select **Financial** in the **navigation list** on the left-hand side.
3. In the pane above, select **Excel Reports**.
4. Double-click the selection marked **TWO AccountTransactions.** The type should be **Data Connection.**

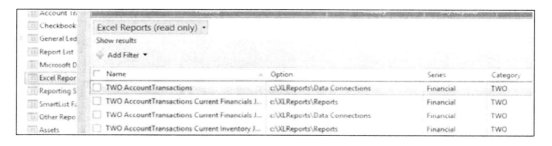

5. Scroll all the way to the right-hand side of the resulting Excel file. You should see two columns labeled **Account Index for Drillback** and **Journal Entry for Drillback**. These are the two default drill downs URLs for journal entry transactions:

   ° **Account Index for Drillback**: This entry will open the **Account Maintenance** window for this account. That's not terribly helpful in most cases since it just lists the account setup.

   ° **Account Index for Journal**: This entry will open the **Journal Entry Inquiry** window for posted transactions and the **Transaction Entry** window for unposted entries. Both of these windows then allow drill back into additional detail.

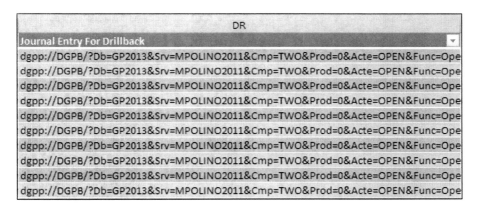

We have the link details, but it's not yet a link in Dynamics GP. To build a formula-based link in Excel 2013, follow these steps:

1. In the Excel sheet, insert a column between columns A and B to create a blank column B.

2. In cell B1, type `JE Link`.

3. In cell B2, type `=HYPERLINK(DR2,A2)`. Cell DR2 should be the first cell under **Journal Entry for Drillback**. Here, we're building a hyperlink using a formula instead of the interface. Unlike the interface-based link we used for revenue, a formula-based link is dynamic, making it easy to build a link per line.

4. Column B now contains the **Journal Entry** number with a link.

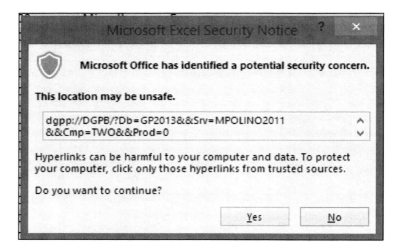

	A	B	C	D	E
	Journal Entry	JE Link	Series	TRX Date	Account Number
1					
2	1543	1543	Financial	5/8/2017	000-1100-00
3	1546	1546	Purchasing	2/15/2017	000-1100-00
4	1545	1545	Purchasing	2/15/2017	000-2111-00
5	1545	1545	Purchasing	2/15/2017	000-1300-01
6	1543	1543	Financial	5/8/2017	000-1100-00
7	1544	1544	Financial	5/9/2017	000-6400-00

5. Scroll down to journal entry **27** and click on the link.

6. Click on **Yes** when the security notice appears.

> **Microsoft Excel Security Notice**   ?   ×
>
> 🛡 **Microsoft Office has identified a potential security concern.**
>
> **This location may be unsafe.**
>
> dgpp://DGPB/?Db=GP2013&&Srv=MPOLINO2011 &&Cmp=TWO&&Prod=0
>
> Hyperlinks can be harmful to your computer and data. To protect your computer, click only those hyperlinks from trusted sources.
>
> Do you want to continue?
>
> Yes   No

 There is a way to disable this box using a registry entry, but there are variations based on your version of Windows and Office. You can find out more at http://www.msoutlook. info/question/245. Make sure to back up the registry before making changes.

7. The **Journal Entry Inquiry** window will open for journal entry **27**. A user can then click on **Source Document** to continue drilling back into the source of this journal entry.

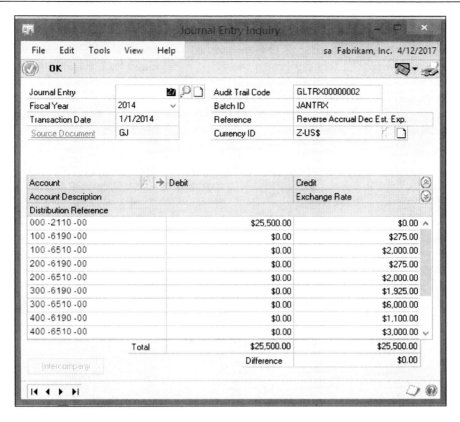

The reason that we selected journal entry **27** to drill back into is that this is a posted journal entry. If we had selected an unposted journal entry, the **Transaction Entry** window would have opened. In the Dynamics GP interface, you can't use an inquiry window to inquire on an unposted journal entry. You get an error message that says that entry hasn't been posted. Because of this, the drill down created is different for posted and unposted transactions.

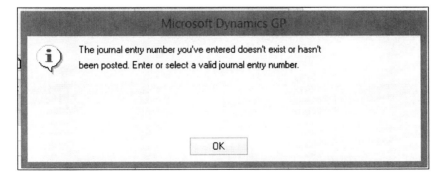

Fixing the journal entry drill down problem

In the release to manufacturing (RTM) version of Dynamics GP 2013, drilling back to an unposted journal entry generates the error message, **The URL was missing required Dynamics GP Drill Back parameters**. There was a change to the way that the URL was structured in GP 2013, and it broke this functionality. There is an "e" in the constant for the action type that shouldn't be there. A fix is due in an upcoming service pack, but if you don't want to wait, there is another option. Executing this SQL code for each GP 2013 company will fix the issue:

```
alter FUNCTION dgppJournalEntry (@action    int,
                                 @JRNENTRY int,
                                 @RCTRXSEQ numeric(19, 5),
                                 @DCSTATUS int,
                                 @DOCTYPE   int)
RETURNS varchar(2000)
AS
  BEGIN
      DECLARE @ActionType   varchar(15),
              @FunctionName varchar(50),
              @URIstring    varchar(255)

      select @FunctionName = 'OpenJournal'

      if @action = 1
        select @ActionType = 'OPEN'
      else
        select @ActionType = 'OPEN'

      select @URIstring = '&Act=' + @ActionType + '&Func=' + @
FunctionName
                          + '&JRNENTRY=' + ltrim(str(@JRNENTRY))
                          + '&RCTRXSEQ=' + ltrim(str(@RCTRXSEQ))
                          + '&DCSTATUS=' + ltrim(str(@DCSTATUS))
                          + '&DOCTYPE=' + ltrim(str(@DOCTYPE))

      RETURN ( @URIstring )
  END
```

Downloading the support files

You can download the code fles for all Packt Publishing books you have purchased from your account at http://www.packtpub.com. You can also download the dashboard application along with the code bundle of this book. If you purchased this book elsewhere, you can visit http://www.packtpub.com/support and register to have the fles e-mailed directly to you.

The code is also available at `https://www.box.com/s/xutg9wbeb9f531cvuevk` (Short link: `http://bit.ly/13VEIr8`).

Drill down link structure

Since we have so much flexibility with drill downs, it's worth understanding what the structure of a drill down looks like.

Here is my drill down link for journal entry **27**:

```
dgpp://DGPB/?Db=GP2013&Srv=MPOLINO2011&Cmp=TWO&Prod=0&Act=OPEN&Func=O
penJournalInq&JRNENTRY=27&RCTRXSEQ=1&YEAR1=2014&TRXDATE=01/01/2014
```

That thing is huge! The good news is that it breaks down pretty easily. All the elements are connected by the ampersand (&) symbol. The description of other elements is given in the following table:

Drill Down elements	Description
`dgpp://DGPB/?`	This is the drill back URL that indicates that the program to work with is Dynamics GP.
`Db=GP2013`	This is the database instance. You won't see a database instance if your GP installation uses the base SQL Server instance. The base instance is more common. In this case, the instance is named GP 2013.
`Srv=MPOLINO2011`	This is the server name. In our example here, the server name is `MPOLINO2011`.
`Cmp=TWO`	`Cmp` represents the database name for the company to drill back to. Our example uses `TWO`, the sample company.
`Prod=0`	This is the product. Product 0 equates to Dynamics GP. Other product numbers might refer to Fixed Assets, Project Accounting, or an ISV solution. Product numbers are listed in the `Dynamics.set` file.
`Act=OPEN`	This is the action, where we are going to open a window.
`Func=OpenJournalInq`	`Func` represents the function. The function we are performing is opening the **Journal Inquiry** window.
`JRNENTRY=27`	This is the first parameter; we want to return Journal Entry 27.

Drill Down elements	Description
`RCTRXSEQ=1`	Recurring Transaction Sequence is the second parameter and it is set to `1`. Since recurring transactions can have the same journal entry, this specifies which instance of a recurring transaction to use.
`TRXDATE=01/01/2014`	The final parameter is the transaction date, January 1, 2014.

Drill down links for inventory, sales, or other transactions will be similar. In our case, the links are already built for us and the link elements are static. Since we know the structure, we can also make the link dynamic and let it get values from a cell.

To illustrate this:

1. Clear column B.

2. Copy and paste the value from cell DR2 into cell B2. It should look like `dgpp://DGPB/?Db=GP2013&Srv=MPOLINO2011&Cmp=TWO&Prod=0&Act=OPEN&Func=OpenJournalInq&JRNENTRY=27&RCTRXSEQ=1&YEAR1=2014&TRXDATE=01/01/2014`.

3. Enclose the entry in quotes.

4. Put an equal sign (=) in front of the first quotation mark to make it a formula.

5. In the **&JRNENTRY=27&** section, change this to be **&JRNENTRY="&A169&"&**.

6. In the **&YEAR1=2014&** section, change this to be **&YEAR1="&BH169&"&**.

7. In the **&TRXDATE=01/01/2014** section, change this to be **&TRXDATE="&TEXT(D169,"mm/dd/yyyy")&"**.

8. The final formula should look like `="dgpp://DGPB/?Db=GP2013&Srv=MPOLINO2011&Cmp=TWO&Prod=0&Act=OPEN&Func=OpenJournalInq&JRNENTRY="&A169&"&RCTRXSEQ=1&YEAR1="&BH169&"&TRXDATE="&TEXT(D169,"mm/dd/yyyy")&""`.

9. Now we have a dynamic formula that gets the appropriate values from the various cells. Note the double quotes at the end to make it all work.

It's time to see how we can apply this practically to our dashboard. We'll take our **Top 10 Customers** tab and enhance it with a drill back to customer information. To do this:

1. Make sure that your `Dashboard.xlsx` file of GP 2013 is open.

2. Select the **Top 10 Customers** tab.

3. Click inside the pivot table. If **Field List** doesn't open on the right-hand side, click on the **Analyze** tab under **PivotTable Tools** and pick **Field List**.

4. In **Field List**, check the box next to **Customer Number**.

5. Uncheck the box next to **Customer Name**.

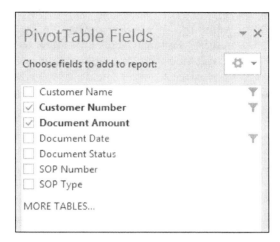

6. Ensure that the pivot table still shows the top 10 customers sorted by **Document Amount**.

7. In cell C3, next to the pivot table header, type `Link`.

8. Save the file.

Okay, everything is prepared. Now, we need to go find the link. To do that, follow these steps:

1. Open Microsoft Dynamics GP 2013.

2. Select **Sales** from the navigation pane on the left-hand side.

3. Pick **Excel Reports** from the navigation list above.

4. In the center, find **Data Connector**, not report, labeled **TWO Customers** and double-click on it.

5. When Excel opens, click on **OK** to put the data in a table.

6. Scroll to the right-hand side in the resulting Excel file to find the column labeled **Customer Number For Drillback**. It should be near column FR.

7. Select the first row below **Customer Number For Drillback**.

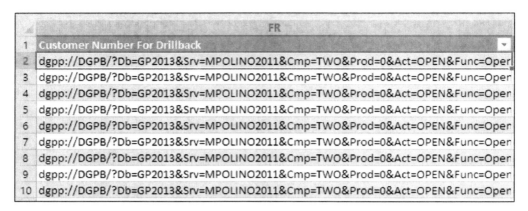

8. Right-click and select **Copy**.
9. Return to the **Top 10 Customers** tab in the Dashboard.xlsx file of GP 2013.
10. Select cell D4.
11. Right-click and pick **Paste**.

	A	B	C	D	E	F
1	Top 10 Customers					
2						
3	**Row Labels** ⬇T	**Sum of Document Amount**	Link			
4	PLAZAONE0001	159,211.89		dgpp://DGPB/?Db=GP2013&Srv		
5	MAHLERST0001	94,697.45				
6	VANCOUVE0001	93,235.36				
7	LAWRENCE0001	93,105.17				
8	ASTORSUI0001	91,846.69				
9	CONTOSOL0001	82,667.53				
10	OFFICEDE0001	74,910.65				
11	VISIONIN0001	73,947.65				
12	BREAKTHR0001	47,321.46				
13	AARONFIT0001	25,171.60				
14	**Grand Total**	**836,115.45**				

12. Click on the link pasted into cell D4.

13. Put an equal sign (=) at the front.

14. Place quotation marks (" ") on the front and back of the link, after the equal sign. It should look similar to `="dgpp://DGPB/?Db=GP2013&Srv=MPOLINO2011&Cmp=TWO&Prod=0&Act=OPEN&Func=OpenCustNmbr&CUSTNMBR=AARONFIT0001"`.

15. At the end of the formula, replace the customer number between the equal sign and the final quote with `"&A4&"`. The final formula should look similar to `="dgpp://DGPB/?Db=GP2013&Srv=MPOLINO2011&Cmp=TWO&Prod=0&Act=OPEN&Func=OpenCustNmbr&CUSTNMBR="&A4&""`.

16. Note that there are two sets of quotes at the end.

17. In cell C4, type the formula, =Hyperlink(D4,"Drillback").

	A	B	C	D	E
1	Top 10 Customers				
2					
3	**Row Labels** ↓T	**Sum of Document Amount**	Link		
4	PLAZAONE0001	159,211.89	Drillback	dgpp://DGPB/?Db=G	
5	MAHLERST0001	94,697.45			
6	VANCOUVE0001	93,235.36			
7	LAWRENCE0001	93,105.17			
8	ASTORSUI0001	91,846.69			
9	CONTOSOL0001	82,667.53			
10	OFFICEDE0001	74,910.65			
11	VISIONIN0001	73,947.65			
12	BREAKTHR0001	47,321.46			
13	AARONFIT0001	25,171.60			
14	**Grand Total**	**836,115.45**			
15					

18. Copy cells C4 and D4 down through all 10 customers.

Top 10 Customers			
Row Labels 🔽	**Sum of Document Amount**	Link	
PLAZAONE0001	159,211.89	Drillback	dgpp://DGPB/?Db=GP2
MAHLERST0001	94,697.45	Drillback	dgpp://DGPB/?Db=GP2
VANCOUVE0001	93,235.36	Drillback	dgpp://DGPB/?Db=GP2
LAWRENCE0001	93,105.17	Drillback	dgpp://DGPB/?Db=GP2
ASTORSUI0001	91,846.69	Drillback	dgpp://DGPB/?Db=GP2
CONTOSOL0001	82,667.53	Drillback	dgpp://DGPB/?Db=GP2
OFFICEDE0001	74,910.65	Drillback	dgpp://DGPB/?Db=GP2
VISIONIN0001	73,947.65	Drillback	dgpp://DGPB/?Db=GP2
BREAKTHR0001	47,321.46	Drillback	dgpp://DGPB/?Db=GP2
AARONFIT0001	25,171.60	Drillback	dgpp://DGPB/?Db=GP2
Grand Total	**836,115.45**		

19. Click one of the drill back links. The **Customer Maintenance** window should open for the customer selected, as shown in the following screenshot:

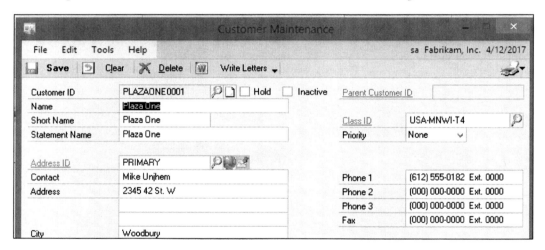

20. With a different drill back, we could link to the **Customer Inquiry** window. We'll clean this up in the next chapter; for now, it all works.

21. Save the file.

Drill Down Builder

Drill Down Builder is part of the optional SmartList Builder product for Microsoft Dynamics GP 2013. SmartList Builder includes:

- SmartList Builder
- Excel Report Builder
- Navigation List Builder
- Drill Down Builder

Drill Down Builder is used to build Drill Down URLs like the ones that we've been using. If you need a Drill Down URL that is not already in an Office Data Connector, Drill Down Builder can be used to create it. With Drill Down Builder, you can even build drill downs back to SmartLists, not just GP 2013 windows.

However, there is one big problem. Drill Down Builder is broken in the initial release of Dynamics GP 2013. We know how it's supposed to work, because it works in Dynamics GP 2010. It broke when Microsoft changed the link format for GP 2013. Microsoft has promised a fix via a service pack, but the problem hasn't been resolved as of this writing.

Once the problem is fixed, there is actually a really good section on Drill Down Builder and the required security in the SmartList Builder User Guide available with Dynamics GP 2013.

The user guide is really unclear on one key point. When you build a drill down with Drill Down Builder, nothing happens when you are done. You have to build an Excel report using Excel Report builder, and add a drill down to the Excel report with the Drill Down button. After that, you need to publish at least the data connection from the Excel report and open it to see the drill down URL.

It's a lot of steps, especially, if you just need to grab a URL for a dashboard, but there's no other way to get a custom drill down URL.

We covered Excel Report Builder earlier in the book in *Chapter 2, The Ultimate GP to Excel Tool: Refreshable Excel Reports*. Creating a drill down is well covered in the SmartList Builder User Guide, so we're going to move on to some complex drill down scenarios.

We would have seen how Drill Down Builder works, but it doesn't work at the moment and the fix may change the behavior from GP 2010.

Complex drill downs

As soon as I show someone drill downs, they get excited, and then the complex scenarios come out. I'll address them here as best I can, but I don't have all the answers yet.

Drilling down with GP 2013 and Excel 2013 on Citrix or Terminal Server

If GP 2013 and Excel 2013 are both running on the same Citrix or Terminal Server instance, drill back from GP 2013 to Excel, as Excel will work as expected. Clicking a drill back link from Excel on Terminal Server or Citrix will open a window in GP 2013 with the appropriate transaction information.

Drilling down to GP 2013 on Citrix with Excel 2013 installed locally

When I originally posted information about drill downs on my blog at `DynamicAccounting.net`, a user wrote back that they managed to get drill downs working with Dynamics GP running on Citrix and Excel installed on the local machine. I can't promise that this will work, but I will offer it here for you as an option to try:

1. Publish the GP Protocol Handler as an application; you must grant permissions to all the same users (and running on the same machines) as GP. Session sharing must be enabled. The command location to publish the GP Protocol Handler is `C:\Program Files (x86)\Common Files\microsoft shared\Dexterity\Microsoft.Dynamics.GP.ProtocolHandler.exe" "%**` (the `%**` is important, and you have to add it manually).

2. On the client machines, you need to create some registry changes. Always back up the registry before making changes and proceed carefully. You'll need to make the following registry entries:

```
[HKEY_CLASSES_ROOT\dgpp]
@="URL: DGPP"
"URL Protocol"=""
[HKEY_CLASSES_ROOT\dgpp\shell]
[HKEY_CLASSES_ROOT\dgpp\shell\open]
[HKEY_CLASSES_ROOT\dgpp\shell\open\command]
```

```
@="\"C:\\Program Files\\Citrix\\ICA Client\\pnagent.exe\" /qlaunch
\"[Farm Name]:[Published App Name]\" /param:\"%1\""
[HKEY_CLASSES_ROOT\dgpp\shell\open\command\ctxvalue]
@="\"C:\\Program Files\\Citrix\\ICA Client\\pnagent.exe\" /qlaunch
\"[Farm Name]:[Published App Name]\" /param:\"%1\""
```

3. [Farm Name] is the name of your XenApp Farm and [Published App Name] is the name you gave to the GP Protocol Handler when you published it in step 1.

Other complex drill down scenarios

I don't have a great answer for this same scenario with Terminal Server, but I suspect that there is an answer for Terminal Server configuration similar to the Citrix setup.

Also, when running GP 2013 as a published app on Citrix or Terminal Server, the setup would be different and finding the answer to that is a work in progress.

As a reminder, drilling back from Excel 2013 to the Dynamics GP 2013 Web Client is not yet supported. This is expected to be added in an upcoming service pack.

Finally, if you restore a production company to a test environment, the server information has already been embedded, even if Excel reports have not been deployed. This means that drill backs will fail, because they are trying to access the production version of Dynamics GP that won't be open. To fix this, you'll need to rebuild the functions, stored procedures, and views in the test company. Fortunately, this isn't as hard as it sounds. To fix drill downs for a copied test company, follow these steps:

1. Log everyone out of Dynamics GP 2013.

2. Access the Database Maintenance Utility with **Start | All Programs | Microsoft Dynamics | GP2013 | Database Maintenance**.

3. In the Database Maintenance Utility, key the SQL server name for the test environment.

4. Check the box next to the company DB that you need to recreate views and procedures for, and click on **Next**.

5. Click on **Mark All** to reload database objects for all products, and click on **Next**.

6. Check the boxes next to both **Functions and Stored Procedures** and **Views,** and click on **Next.**

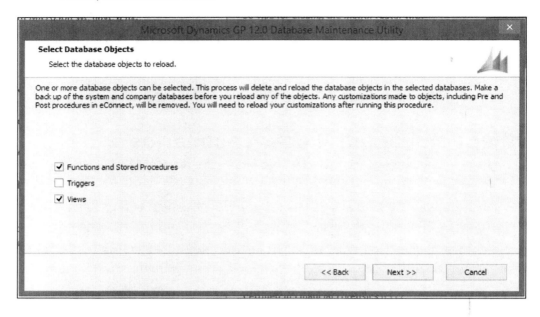

7. Hit **Next** on the confirmation window.
8. A final screen will pop up indicating success. After that you should be able to play with drill downs in your test environment.

Our dashboard is just about done. We have some cleanup to do in the next chapter to really make it look good, so let's wrap things up.

Summary

Despite the problems with Drill Down Builder in the initial release of Dynamics GP 2013, drill down functionality is extremely powerful. Being able to drill back into the information source adds credibility to the dashboard. If users have questions, they can drill back for answers. Hyperlinks provide connectivity to pull supporting data together to enhance the functionality of a dashboard.

In our next chapter, we will really make our dashboard look good by finalizing the look and feel.

8
Bringing it All Together

Over the last several chapters, we've pulled together all the key elements of our Excel 2013-based dashboard from data in Microsoft Dynamics GP 2013. We've gone beyond just a dashboard with supplemental schedules and drill back into Dynamics GP. But, our dashboard is still plain looking. The charts and conditional formatting help, but the dashboard still needs some work to really make it sexy. In this chapter, we'll pull all the elements together to make everything work visually. We will also look at options to make the dashboard available to as many people as possible. Specifically, we're going to cover:

- Headers
- Cleanup
- Logos
- Backgrounds
- Good design
- Deployment options

Adding headers

Our dashboard needs a couple of small elements for it to be complete, and then we'll dress it up. First up, we need the company name and header. Let's add those by following these steps:

1. Open the `Dashboard.xlsx` file of GP 2013 that we've been working with.

2. Our sample company is Fabrikam, so in cell B1 type `Fabrikam`.

3. Change the color to a dark orange and set the font size to **24**.

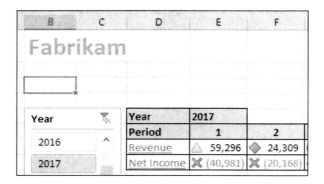

4. In cell B2, type `Financial Dashboard` to label this dashboard.

5. Change the color to a dark blue.

6. Save the file.

Cleaning it up

The titles were the last missing element. While our dashboard has all the elements we want, it still looks like Microsoft Excel. Dashboards are about melding function and form. Our functional elements are done, but we still have some work on the form.

There is one overriding thing that you can do to clean up any Excel-based dashboard. If you do nothing else, please do this one item. That item is turn off the gridlines. Turning off gridlines is the simplest way to give a clean look to Excel data. To turn off gridlines:

1. Select the **Dashboard** tab.

2. Click on **View** on the ribbon.

3. Uncheck the box marked **Gridlines**.

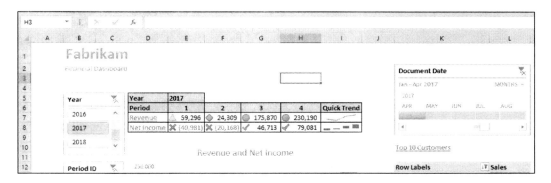

4. Repeat this process for the other tabs.

5. We will clean up the row and column indicators at the end. I'm leaving them in for now to finish up the formatting.

Another key design element for our dashboard is leaving enough space around the dashboard elements. Most Excel users have a reflexive love of cell A1. They feel compelled to put data in column A and row 1, but when you look at other examples of anything graphic-heavy, no one sticks information in the upper-left corner. Our dashboard needs some white space to really make the graphic elements pop. We did a little bit of this by using column B and leaving column A blank. But we need to do this at the top as well. To clean up the dashboard to add some white space, follow these steps:

1. Select the **Dashboard** tab.

2. Select the gray number **1** row indicator on the left-hand side.

3. Right-click and select **Insert Row**.

4. Now select the **Revenue** tab.

5. Select the gray number **1** row indicator on the left-hand side.

6. Right-click and select **Insert Row**.

7. Select the gray column **A** row indicator on top.

8. Right-click and select **Insert Column**.

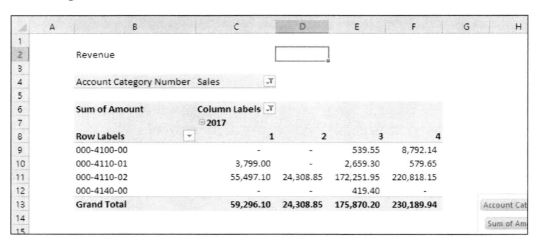

9. Repeat this process for all the other tabs.

10. For all the tabs, except the **Dashboard** tab, go back through one more time and set the size of each title in B2 to **14**.

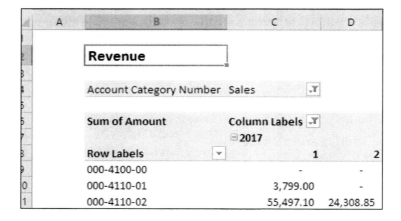

11. Return to the **Dashboard** tab.

12. Save the file. In the last chapter, we added some drill backs to our **Top 10 Customers** tab. The drill back links are pretty messy, so let's clean them up. We have two options to hide our drill downs. We can make them invisible or we can hide the column. My preference is to hide the column, but we'll look at both.

Top 10 Customers

Row Labels	↓T Sum of Document Amount	Link		
PLAZAONE0001	159,211.89	Drillback	dgpp://DGPB/?Db=GP	
MAHLERST0001	94,697.45	Drillback	dgpp://DGPB/?Db=GP	
VANCOUVE0001	93,235.36	Drillback	dgpp://DGPB/?Db=GP	
LAWRENCE0001	93,105.17	Drillback	dgpp://DGPB/?Db=GP	
ASTORSUI0001	91,846.69	Drillback	dgpp://DGPB/?Db=GP	
CONTOSOL0001	82,667.53	Drillback	dgpp://DGPB/?Db=GP	
OFFICEDE0001	74,910.65	Drillback	dgpp://DGPB/?Db=GP	
VISIONIN0001	73,947.65	Drillback	dgpp://DGPB/?Db=GP	
BREAKTHR0001	47,321.46	Drillback	dgpp://DGPB/?Db=GP	
AARONFIT0001	25,171.60	Drillback	dgpp://DGPB/?Db=GP	
Grand Total	**836,115.45**			

To make the drill back links invisible:

1. Select the **Top 10 Customers** tab.
2. Highlight the drill backs in cells E5 through E14.
3. Use the **Font Color** icon to make the font color white.
4. Use the **Fill Color** icon (paint bucket) to make the background white.
5. Ensure that any cell borders are turned off.

This process effectively blends these fields into the background. The risk with this method is that the fields can get overwritten. That would break the drill down.

To hide the column containing the drill down:

1. Select the **Top 10 Customers** tab.
2. Highlight the gray column **E** header.

3. Right-click and select **Hide**.

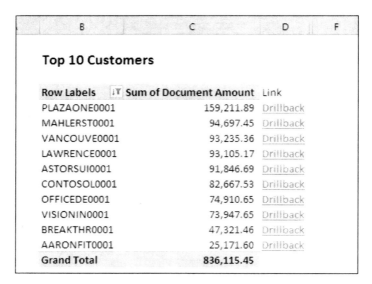

To bring this column back to making changes:

1. Highlight the column **D** through **F** headers.
2. Right-click and select **Unhide**.

We've built links from the dashboard to some of the supplemental tabs in the workbook. Let's go ahead and round out links to the other tabs. We need to add links to **Receivables** and to our **Sales by City** tabs. The **Cash** tab doesn't really add much value, and it is used solely for the speedometer chart, so we'll hide that tab from users.

To link **Receivables** and **Sales by City** to our dashboard:

1. Select the **Dashboard** tab.
2. Scroll down to cell K26, just above the **Receivables** chart.
3. Type Receivables in the cell.
4. Select **Insert | Hyperlink**.
5. Select **Place in This Document** on the left-hand side.
6. Pick **Receivables Aging** and click on **OK**.

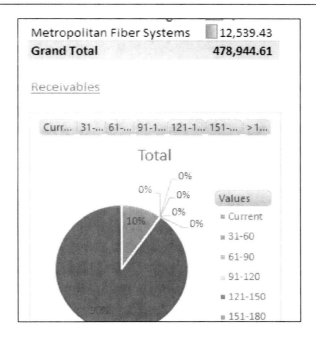

7. Select cell L11 on the **Dashboard** tab. This is the cell immediately to the right-hand side of the **Top 10 Customers** link.

8. Type `Sales by City` in the cell.

9. Select **Insert | Hyperlink**.

10. Select **Place in This Document** on the left-hand side.

11. Pick **Sales by City** and click **OK**.

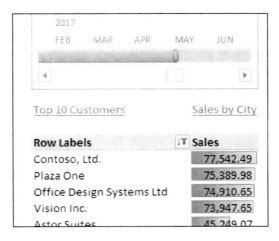

To hide the **Cash** tab:

1. Right-click on the **Cash** tab.
2. Click on **Hide**.

 It's tempting to hide tabs to provide as clean a dashboard as possible. Remember, though, if a tab is hidden, any hyperlinks pointing to that tab won't work. Hyperlinks can't open a hidden tab.

To unhide the **Cash** tab to make adjustments:

1. Right-click on any tab.
2. Click on **Unhide**.
3. Select the sheet to unhide and click on **OK**.

While these links are helpful, once the user gets to the supplemental information, it's important to give them a way to get back to the main dashboard. This makes the dashboard act more like an application and less like a dashboard. To link back to the dashboard:

1. Select the **Revenue** tab.
2. Place the cursor in cell F2.
3. Type `Return to Dashboard`.
4. Select **Insert | Hyperlink**.
5. Select **Place in This Document** on the left-hand side.
6. Pick **Dashboard** and click on **OK**.

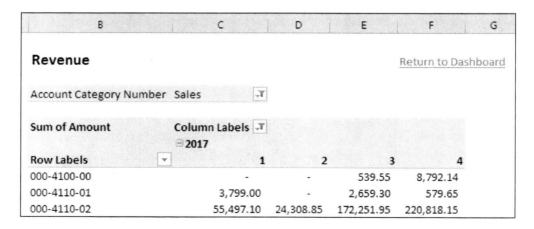

7. Copy cell E2 from the **Revenue** tab to all the other tabs except the **Dashboard** and **Sales by City** tabs. **Sales by City** is the PowerView-based tab, and it doesn't work like the others. There is no simple way to link back from this tab.

Now that all of our information is linked together, let's make it all look good.

Adding a logo

In almost every case, you'll want to add a company logo to the dashboard. Logos help dress up even a plain dashboard. Often they end up in the left-hand corner, so you may need to move your titles around. They don't have to end up there though.

For our example, I wanted something available to every Excel user, so we'll use a star symbol available in Excel 2013 as our company logo.

To add our sample logo, follow these steps:

1. Select the **Dashboard** tab.
2. On the ribbon, select **Insert | Pictures Online**.
3. In the **Office Clip Art** search box, type Gold Star and hit *Enter*.
4. Select the first gold star on the left-hand side and click on **Insert**.

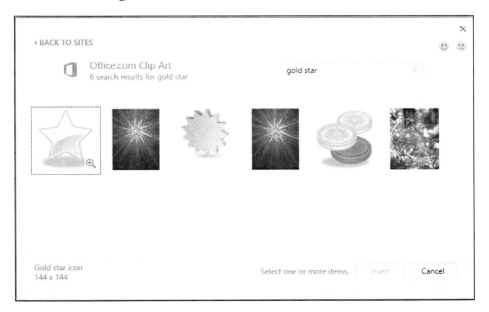

5. Drag the star into the area under column **H** at the top of the sheet.

6. Use the handles to resize the star to fit in the white space below column **H**.

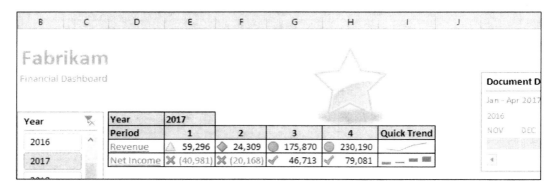

For your company logo, your process will typically be slightly different. I needed a graphic that everyone has access to. Your process will probably look more like the following steps:

1. Select the **Dashboard** tab.
2. On the ribbon, select **Insert | Pictures**.
3. Use the explorer window to find the appropriate logo.
4. Select the logo and click on **Insert**.
5. Resize and position the logo as appropriate.

Often, this is where people stop when formatting any Excel workbook. Right now, it's just okay. The sheet is at least clean, but it doesn't have that wow factor just yet. Even with a clean sheet, the white background is boring. Let's spice things up with some color.

Creating backgrounds

Backgrounds provide a way to really distance the user from the fact that this is Excel. They allow the user to ignore the vessel and focus on the content. There are really three options for creating a background in Excel 2013. They aren't mutually exclusive, and sometimes, combining options can be the best solution. The three options are:

- A color background using **Fill Color**
- A picture background using **Insert Picture**
- A picture background using Excel's **Background** feature

We'll look at each of these and how they can be used together. Up first, **Fill Color**.

The Fill Color feature

With the **Fill Color** feature, we're simply going to apply a background color to all the cells. If nothing else, this helps dampen the bright white background. It can also be used to really offset certain items.

To add a background color:

1. Select the **Dashboard** tab.
2. Click on the gray header cell between **A** and **1** (it resembles a down arrow) to select the entire sheet.
3. Click on the drop-down next to the paint bucket icon in the font area of the **Home** ribbon.
4. Highlight different colors to see how they affect the background. Lighter colors tend to work better.
5. Select a light-blue color for our background for now. Notice how the white charts pop against a contrasting background. Let's make the **Revenue and Net Income** section stand out as well.
6. Highlight the cells D7 through I9.
7. Click the drop-down next to the paint bucket item again and select **No Fill**.
8. Repeat this for cells D6 and E6.

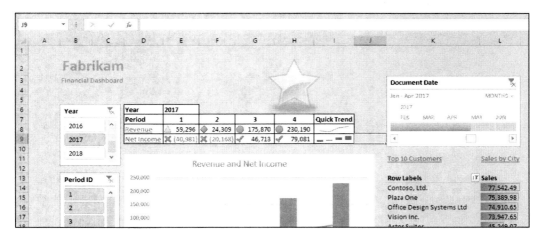

Now the **Revenue and Net Income** section contrasts nicely with the blue background.

Inserting a picture

Another way to set up a background is to insert a picture. This process is similar to inserting our logo. There are pros and cons to inserting a picture this way, but first, let's see how to do it.

1. Select the **Dashboard** tab.

2. Click on **Insert | Online Pictures**.

3. Next to **Office.com Clip Art**, type `Blue Star` and hit *Enter*.

4. Select the pattern with just blue stars.

5. Click on **Insert**.

6. Drag the image with the stars to cell A1.

7. Use the handles to resize the stars to fit in cells A1 to L12. This will cover up part of the dashboard.

8. Right-click on the star graphic and select **Send to back**.

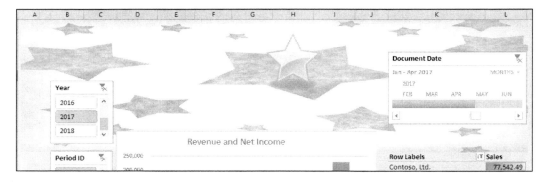

9. Notice that when we send the graphic to the back, slicers, charts, and other graphic elements can sit on top of the picture. However, Excel text and pivot tables cannot.

10. Resize the picture to fit in cells D2 through L5.

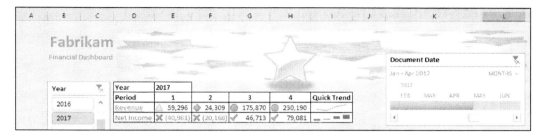

Like the logo, we used a picture from Online Pictures to ensure that the graphic is available to everyone. You would typically use **Pictures** on the **Insert** menu.

Pictures inserted this way can't sit behind non-graphical items. They hide the Excel-based text. This is one of the limitations of using **Insert Picture**. By resizing the picture so that it only fits behind graphical elements, we can use a picture as a header and still apply it to the dashboard. This isn't the best picture to illustrate this. A long, banner-like graphic would be better, but I think you get the idea. You'll notice that adding a picture didn't interfere with our colored background. In fact, it added to it.

Before we move on, select the picture graphic and hit *Delete* to remove it.

Inserting a background

This method is one that most people don't know whether it exists in Microsoft Excel. Excel 2013 has the ability to add a background picture behind a sheet. Excel text and graphic elements flow over the background. One limitation of this method is that the background is repeated over and over. There isn't a way to just show the background graphic once. Additionally, if there is a colored background, it will overlay and hide the background graphic. Let's see how to create a background by following these steps:

1. Select the **Dashboard** tab.

2. Click the gray header cell between **A** and **1** (it resembles a down arrow) to select the entire sheet.

3. On the **Home** ribbon, click on the drop-down next to the **Fill Color** (paint bucket) icon.

4. Select **No Fill** to clear the background color.

5. Pick **Page Layout | Background** on the ribbon.

6. In the **Office.com Clip Art** search box, type Blue Star.

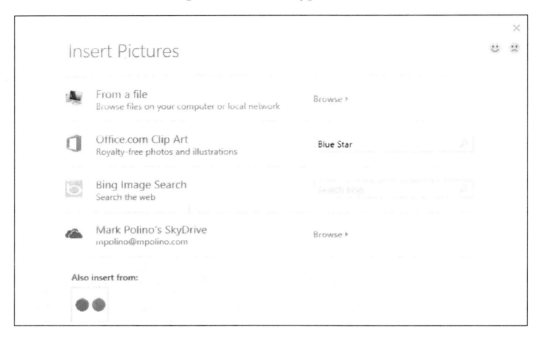

7. Pick the background with just blue stars and hit *Insert*.

8. The blue star background fills in behind the other elements.

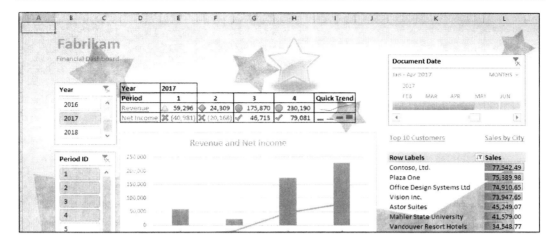

9. Save the file.

> I want to point out that we've built a pretty good-looking, fully refreshable dashboard connected to Dynamics GP 2013, and we haven't used a single macro. We haven't written a line of Visual Basic code, and the resulting Microsoft Excel 2013 file is a basic XLSX file, not a macro-based Excel file.

Our dashboard is done except for hiding a few elements that we'll cover at the end. You are free to repeat any of these looks on the supporting schedules. I tend to make the main dashboard the best looking and go a little plainer with the supporting schedules, but feel free to experiment.

Good design

In our example dashboard, we're limited in the graphics that are available to us. I wanted to use pictures that are available to the widest number of users. But, I also don't want you to be limited to what everyone else does. If you use Google or Bing to look up images of Excel-based dashboards, they all quickly start to look alike. We're going to look at a different example to help provide some inspiration.

Author Tyler Chessman has written a book on the U.S. national debt. The book is appropriately titled *Understanding the United States Debt*. What's really cool for us is that Tyler has taken the U.S. national debt and broken it down in Excel using all the elements that we've used for our dashboard. It is, without a doubt, the best looking Excel dashboard that I've ever seen.

The debt data is loaded via PowerPivot, which we look at in the next chapter, and the Excel sheet is available for download at `http://understandingtheusdebt.com/data.aspx`.

This fantastic dashboard looks like the following screenshot:

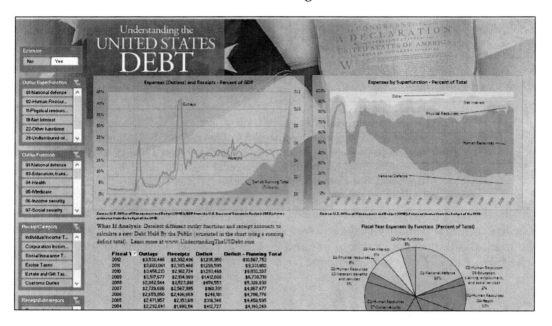

This dashboard uses charts and pivot tables to display various debt elements.

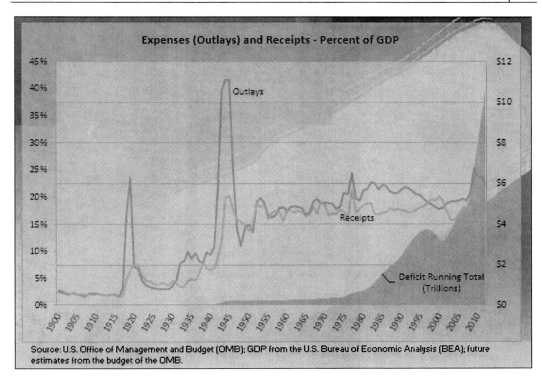

Source: U.S. Office of Management and Budget (OMB); GDP from the U.S. Bureau of Economic Analysis (BEA); future estimates from the budget of the OMB.

The elements in this dashboard aren't special. It uses the same charts, pivot tables, and conditional formatting that we've been working with.

Fiscal Year	Outlays	Receipts	Deficit	Deficit - Running Total
2012	$3,538,446	$2,302,496	$1,235,950	$10,567,752
2011	$3,603,061	$2,303,466	$1,299,595	$9,331,802
2010	$3,456,213	$2,162,724	$1,293,489	$8,032,207
2009	$3,517,677	$2,104,989	$1,412,688	$6,738,718
2008	$2,982,544	$2,523,991	$458,553	$5,326,030
2007	$2,728,686	$2,567,985	$160,701	$4,867,477
2006	$2,655,050	$2,406,869	$248,181	$4,706,776
2005	$2,471,957	$2,153,611	$318,346	$4,458,595
2004	$2,292,841	$1,880,114	$412,727	$4,140,249
2003	$2,159,899	$1,782,314	$377,585	$3,727,522
2002	$2,010,894	$1,853,136	$157,758	$3,349,937

Slicers give end users control over the different debt elements.

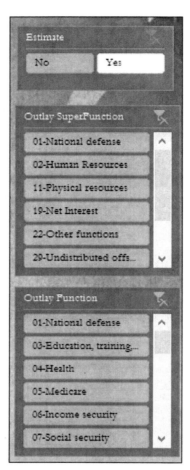

A picture was inserted at the top as a header.

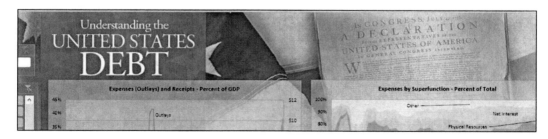

Only graphical elements, charts, and slicers overlap the heading picture. When the heading picture ends, a complementary color fill is used to blend the heading into the rest of the dashboard.

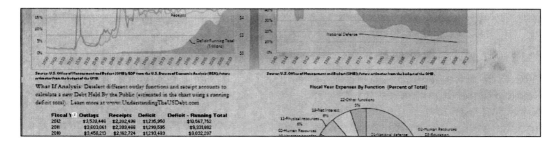

Conditional formatting is used in some tabs to highlight items.

USNumberOfEmployees_NotSeasAdj	Column Labels			
Row Labels	1900	1910	1920	1930
⊟ Private	98.85%	98.54%	97.79%	91.54%
⊟ Goods-producing	50.07%	50.28%	47.57%	38.97%
⊞ Mining and logging	4.54%	5.24%	4.69%	3.15%
⊞ Construction	9.09%	8.26%	5.05%	7.51%
⊞ Manufacturing	33.77%	34.11%	35.18%	25.81%
⊞ Goods-producing, other	2.67%	2.66%	2.64%	2.50%
⊟ Private service-providing	48.78%	48.26%	50.23%	52.56%
⊞ Trade, transportation, and utilities	26.92%	27.52%	29.31%	29.70%
⊞ Information	0.00%	0.00%	0.00%	0.00%
⊞ Financial activities	0.00%	0.00%	0.00%	0.00%
⊞ Professional and business services	0.00%	0.00%	0.00%	0.00%

This Excel sheet only has five tabs. All of them are visible at the bottom. The author doesn't link the sheets, perhaps because there are only five of them, but that is about the only one of our elements that is not present in this dashboard.

I have a couple of points in walking you through this example:

- All the tools we used in our example are used here to make a gorgeous dashboard.

- The magic is not in the elements, it's in how you put them together. Once you have the data, get creative.

- If someone can make something as ugly as the U.S. national debt look this good, imagine what you could do with your company's financial data.

Final cleanup

When you are sure that you have the dashboard you want, there are a couple of final cleanup items. It's often helpful to turn off Excel Headings and the Formula Bar. It can be helpful to hide the ribbon. One caution though: if you need to make changes, you'll find that you need to turn these on again to really get anything done. Make sure that you are done with changes before taking these steps.

Headings are the column and row letters and numbers. Turning them off really makes the Excel look and feel disappear. To turn off headings:

1. Select **View** on the ribbon.

2. Uncheck the box next to **Headings**.

3. Repeat this process for each tab.

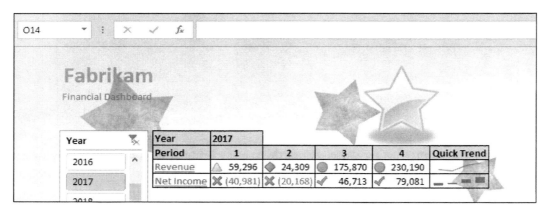

Gridlines and Headings can be turned on and off for each tab. The formula bar is universal. It's either on or off. If you turn it off, it's off for all the tabs. To turn off the formula bar:

1. Select **View** on the ribbon.

2. Uncheck the box next to **Formula Bar**.

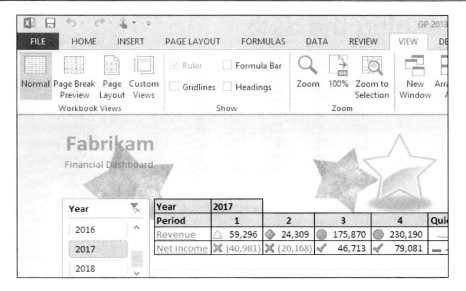

Finally, we can hide the ribbon for the full application effect. To hide the ribbon, follow these steps:

1. In the upper-right, next to the help icon (?), select the icon that looks like a box with an up arrow.

2. Pick **Auto-hide Ribbon** from the choices.

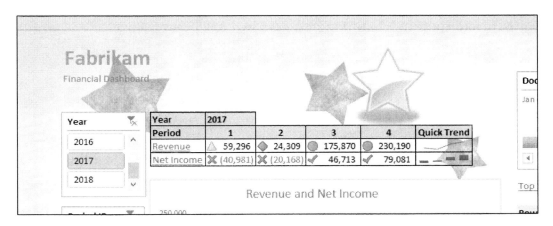

You can unhide the ribbon by clicking the same icon and picking **Show Tabs and Commands**.

Refreshing the data

One problem with hiding the ribbon is that it makes it hard for the user to refresh the data. Certainly the **Refresh data when opening the file** or the **Refresh every XX minutes** settings in the data sources can help with that, but there are plenty of good reasons for a user to want to be able to refresh data on demand. Selecting *Alt + F5* with the keyboard will also refresh all, so that is an option when the ribbon is hidden.

You can put a note in the sheet to remind folks how to complete an on-demand refresh with the button or with *Alt + F5*. We've tried to minimize the effort on the part of the user, but we are asking users to interpret and make decisions based on data in this dashboard. Learning to click on the **Refresh All** or a simple keystroke combination button should be within their skill set.

Sharing

Now we've built this great dashboard. We can refresh it and see the latest numbers at will. Rarely are we the only users of our dashboard. We've built this dashboard to support the organization, and we've built it in a way that is easy to use and understand. Now we have to figure out how to make it available to more users. There are a number of options available. We will explore the various options, but some of them can be quite complex, so we won't go into them in detail. In the real world, if you've got a great dashboard, and it makes the Controller and/or the CFO happy, you'll get the resources to get it deployed.

Some common options for sharing an Excel-based dashboard include:

- E-mail
- Network sharing
- Hosting via SkyDrive
- Downloading via SkyDrive
- Downloading via SharePoint
- Hosting via SharePoint Excel Services
- Hosting with PowerPivot

We will look at each of these quickly.

The quick option – e-mail

E-mail is still the most common way to share an Excel-based dashboard, certainly at the start. One of the benefits of our dashboard is that if the users we e-mail it to are on the network and have appropriate security, we don't have to send it to them repeatedly. The users can simply save the dashboard and refresh it. However, if you make structural changes to the dashboard, you will need to resend it. This can result in users having different versions of the dashboard. Usually, that's not a good thing.

Whether or not users can update a dashboard delivered via e-mail depends on a couple of factors. If the connection is embedded in the spreadsheet, and the user has access to the source via the network, VPN, or some other method, they should be able to update it. If the connection is embedded in an **Office Data Connection** (**ODC**) file, the ODC file may need to travel with the spreadsheet as well.

Network sharing

Typically, the next step is to place the dashboard in a shared network location. This ensures that all users are using the same versions. Any new versions would overwrite the old ones, keeping everyone up to date.

Hosting via SkyDrive

SkyDrive is one of Microsoft's cloud options for file storage and access. Documents stored on SkyDrive can be opened via Excel on the Web. Before you get all excited that this is the answer you've been looking for, you also need to understand that there are a lot of limitations. These include:

- There is a maximum file size when opening an Excel file. Microsoft continues to increase the size, but it's still relatively easy to hit the limit.
- Many dashboard elements won't work on the web version of Excel.
- Users won't be able to refresh data from Dynamics GP using SkyDrive.

These limitations are pretty severe, but there are scenarios where it makes sense to publish a static version of a dashboard for remote locations and host the file on SkyDrive.

Downloading via SkyDrive

SkyDrive can also be used to download an Excel file, much like a network location. File sizes typically aren't an issue, but again, without a connection back to Dynamics GP, these files can't be refreshed. However, we've looked at a number of techniques for building dashboards. Some of them included embedding data in the file. While this isn't preferred, it could be used to give remote users a regularly updated dashboard to work with, especially if the analysis only requires periodic data, such as monthly financial information.

Downloading via SharePoint

A step that many companies take after they try the downloading from the network option is to move the file into SharePoint and let users download from there. SharePoint provides options such as version control and even more extensive security. This is really just a tiny step-up from downloading from the network. Users still download the file and run it locally, and users still need appropriate access to update the dashboard.

Hosting via SharePoint Excel Services

Now we start to approach the answer that most folks are looking for. Excel Services is a SharePoint technology that allows users to make Excel workbooks available via SharePoint. End users don't need to have Microsoft Excel on their machines. The information is actually displayed using Excel Services, not using Microsoft Excel 2013. Files can be uploaded, secured, displayed, refreshed, and shared via Excel Services on SharePoint. Microsoft's Office 365 cloud offering contains similar functionality to make Excel data available to users online and refreshable by the user.

Summary

That's it, we've built a pretty nice dashboard. It connects to Dynamics GP 2013; it's refreshable and portable. You can do the same thing for your company. The core is just the basic building blocks of pivot tables, conditional formatting, and charts.

But wait, we're not done! In the next chapter, we'll look at how to go even farther with your dashboard using new PowerPivot functionality built into Microsoft Excel 2013, and we still have to explore some more exotic options.

9
Expanding Pivot Tables with PowerPivot

We've finished our dashboard, then why is there more book left? Because of PowerPivot, of course! PowerPivot is a data summarization and exploration tool now built into Microsoft Excel 2013. This is the future of Excel-based analytics. After you've built a few dashboards, you'll be ready for the next level, and PowerPivot is the next level, so I'm giving you a look at it here.

PowerPivot started as a free, downloadable add-in for Excel 2010 from the SQL Server team. It has grown into a full-fledged member of the Excel 2013 feature set. There is a lot of overlap between PowerPivot and regular Excel pivot tables. Both allow users to analyze data via pivot tables and charts. Both can use data from inside or outside of Microsoft Excel.

So, what's so special about PowerPivot? It's special in a couple of different ways, specifically:

- PowerPivot uses an in-memory analytics engine, dubbed xVelocity, to let users work with pivot tables based on millions of rows. This is a lot more information than could ever fit into an Excel worksheet. Where Excel slows down with pivot tables based on a couple of hundred thousand rows, PowerPivot keeps on going, even with millions of rows or hundreds of millions of rows if your hardware can handle it.

- PowerPivot provides options to connect multiple sources as if they were relational tables. These are things such as an Excel spreadsheet, a SQL table, and a text file. Excel 2013 adds the ability to connect multiple sources via the new Excel Data Model feature, but it's really PowerPivot managing the connections behind the scenes.

- Trying to reproduce the flexibility of PowerPivot in Excel would require a wild combination of vlookup formulas and calculations to flatten multiple data sources into a single table that could then be pulled into an Excel PivotTable.

- PowerPivot provides its own set of formulas known as **Data Analysis Expression Language (DAX)**. DAX formulas are very similar to Excel formulas, making them easy to learn, but when it comes to manipulating data, they can be more powerful than classic Excel formulas.

- Some of you are thinking that PowerPivot seems pretty technical as well as powerful. After all, you're just an accountant, right? This is wrong, of course. The value in accounting comes from understanding and interpreting information, not keying debits and credits. In September 2011, PowerPivot had its coming-out party for accountants. The Journal of Accountancy put out a feature article (not a technical column) on PowerPivot and its value to accountants. That was before the added features in Excel 2013. The Journal article is available on the Web at `http://www.journalofaccountancy.com/Issues/2011/Sep/20113876.htm`. If you haven't heard of PowerPivot before now, you're already behind.

> With the final release of Excel 2013, Microsoft made a licensing change around PowerPivot. PowerPivot and PowerView are now only available in the Office 2013 Professional Plus version. The "Plus" is the important part. Most companies using volume licensing will have Professional Plus, but smaller organizations or students that acquire Office 2013 at retail won't get PowerPivot. Excel professionals have lobbied Microsoft to get this changed, but for now, you need the Professional Plus version.

Since you need to understand the basics of PowerPivot, in this chapter, you'll learn about:

- Power Pivot Basics
- Bringing data into PowerPivot via:
  - Text
  - Excel files
  - SQL Server
- Pivot table creation with PowerPivot

- New data options including:
  - Atom feeds
  - SSRS Reports
  - Azure Marketplace

- More PowerPivot capabilities

PowerPivot Basics

When you fire up Excel 2013, there is a new ribbon titled **PowerPivot**. Clicking on **Manage** opens up the main PowerPivot window. This isn't really an Excel window, even though it's open in Excel. Most of the PowerPivot work takes place in this window. PowerPivot has its own set of menus that appear in the PowerPivot window.

Closing the PowerPivot window returns you to Excel. This can be a little disconcerting the first time. Users are often worried that they are closing the full Excel workbook.

Now that we've looked at the basics, let's look at some options to bring information into PowerPivot.

Bringing Dynamics GP 2013 information to PowerPivot

With Excel 2013, PowerPivot is now included and not a separate download. Parts of it still exist as an included add-on, and it definitely behaves a little differently than the Excel you used. For example, you can't key data directly into a PowerPivot sheet, and you can't change information that's been brought in.

Since we can't key data into PowerPivot, we have to get it there somehow. For GP data, there are a couple of commonly used options. These include:

- Copying and pasting
- Linking to a spreadsheet
- Connecting via SQL Server

We will look at all three of these variants.

Copying and pasting

Sometimes you need to just get data into PowerPivot. Maybe it's a small amount that another source will use to look up information, like clarifying that 1 equals `True` and 2 equals `False`. Maybe the data source is in a place that is hard to connect to because of security constraints, physical location, or network controls. Whatever the reason, copying and pasting information is about as easy as it gets. For our illustration, we're going to use the account summary Excel report that we've been working with. Typically, we would want to connect this directly to SQL server, like we'll look at later in the chapter. However, there are lots of cases where you get a spreadsheet or file with no connection to the source, so think of this as an example, not necessarily a best practice.

To illustrate how to copy and paste data into PowerPivot, follow these steps:

1. Open Microsoft Dynamics GP 2013.

2. In Dynamics GP, on the navigation pane, on the left-hand side, click on **Financial**. The list pane above will change to show financial items.

3. In the list pane, click on **Excel Reports**.

4. In the navigation list in the center, select **TWO Account Summary Default**. Make sure that you select **Option** that includes **Reports**.

5. Double-click on the **TWO Account Summary Default** item.

6. Once the file opens in Excel 2013, place your cursor in cell A1.

7. Right-click and select **Table | Convert to Range**. Click on **OK** when the warning opens. PowerPivot won't copy and paste properly if the data is in a table.

8. Select *Ctrl + Shift + End* to highlight the account summary data.

9. Right-click and select **Copy**.

10. In Excel, select the **PowerPivot** tab and then go to **Manage | Paste**.

11. Name the table `Account Summary`, and make sure that the box labeled **Use first row as column headers** is checked. Click on **OK**.

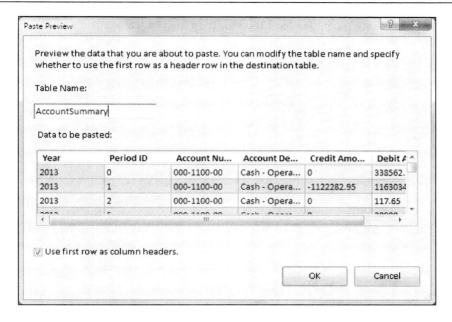

Like Excel worksheet columns, we can move columns around and add columns of calculated fields to the end of our data. As an example, let's add a quick formula by following these steps:

1. Grab the **Debit Amount** column with your mouse and drag it to the left-hand side of the **Credit Amount** column.

2. In the box below **Add Column**, type the equals sign (=). All PowerPivot formulas have to start with an equals sign.

3. With your mouse, select the field immediately below the **Debit Amount** heading. PowerPivot will start to build a formula just like Excel does.

4. Key the minus sign (-), and select the field below the **Credit Amount** heading, then hit *Enter*.

5. Save this file to your desktop as PowerPivotSample.xlsx. We'll use it again in just a minute.

6. Just like working with Excel tables, the result of the formula will be copied down.

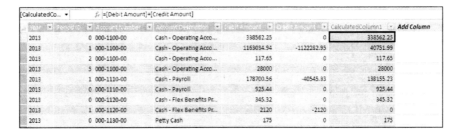

Copying and pasting is a great option for data that's not going to change much over time or data that can be difficult to retrieve. Next we're going to look at adding data to PowerPivot by linking to an Excel sheet.

Linking to a spreadsheet

Another easy way to get data into PowerPivot is with an Excel sheet. It's not uncommon to find supplemental information scattered in spreadsheets throughout an organization. Having an option to tie these spreadsheets with Dynamics GP 2013 data can be a huge help towards getting a more comprehensive view of a company's information.

Adding an Excel sheet from the current workbook into PowerPivot is actually really easy, so let's see what it looks like by following these steps:

1. Open Microsoft Dynamics GP 2013.

2. In Dynamics GP, on the navigation pane, on the left-hand side, click on **Financial**. The list pane above will change to show financial items.

3. In the list pane, click on **Excel Reports**.

4. In the navigation list, in the center, select **TWO Accounts Default**. Make sure that you select **Option** that includes **Reports**.

5. Double-click on the **TWO Accounts Default** item.

6. Once the file opens in Excel 2013, select **PowerPivot | Add to Data Model**.

7. That's it. The current Excel data is now available in PowerPivot.

8. Close the Excel file without saving. We've got some other examples to work through.

What if the Excel data you need is in a different Excel file? What if you want to bring two Excel files into PowerPivot? There's no problem doing so. You don't have to copy data into Excel or manually combine Excel files the old way. Let's look at combining different files. To illustrate this, we will use the `PowerPivotSample.xlsx` that we saved earlier and a saved Excel file. Let's combine these files.

First, we need to create and save an Excel file. To get our Excel file, follow these steps:

1. Open Microsoft Dynamics GP 2013.

2. In Dynamics GP, on the navigation pane, on the left-hand side, click on **Financial**. The list pane above will change to show financial items.

3. In the list pane, click on **Excel Reports**.

4. In the navigation list, in the center, select **TWO Accounts Default**. Make sure that you select **Option** that includes **Reports**.

5. Double-click on the **TWO Accounts Default** item.

6. When Excel 2013 opens, right-click inside the data, and select **Table | Convert to Range**. Click on **OK** when the warning opens.

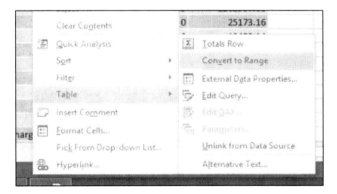

7. Save the file to your desktop as `TWO Accounts Default.xlsx` and close the file.

Now let's combine these in PowerPivot by following these steps:

1. Open `PowerPivotSample.xlsx` from your desktop.

2. Select **PowerPivot | Manage | From Other Sources**.

3. Scroll down and select **Excel File,** then click on **Next**.

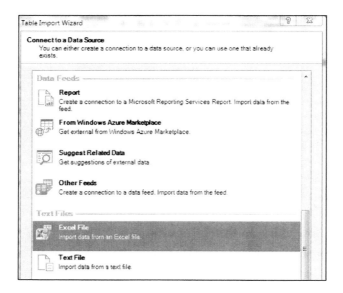

4. Click on the **Browse** button and navigate to your desktop.

5. Select the TWO Accounts Default.xlsx file and click on **Open**.

6. Check the **Use first row as column headers** checkbox and click on **Next**.

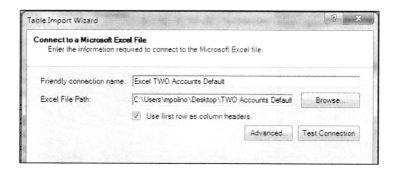

7. Check the box next to **'Accounts Default$'**.

8. Click on **Finish** and then on **Close**.

9. A new tab gets created in PowerPivot with the **TWO Accounts Default** data.

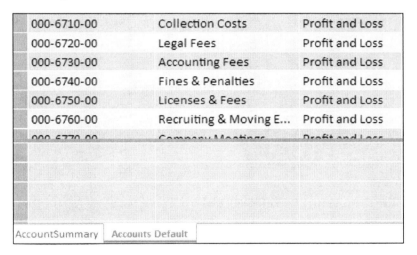

Now we have two sets of data in PowerPivot, but if we want to create a pivot table to analyze this data, we need to connect the data in much the same way we join SQL tables together. Don't miss how powerful it can be to connect things such as text data from a report, Excel data from another system, and SQL server data from Dynamics GP. Even more importantly, you don't have to be a data integration specialist to make it happen. To join these two datasets, follow these steps:

1. In the PowerPivot for Excel window, click on the **AccountSummary** tab.
2. Select **Design | Create Relationship**.
3. The **Create Relationship** box will open.

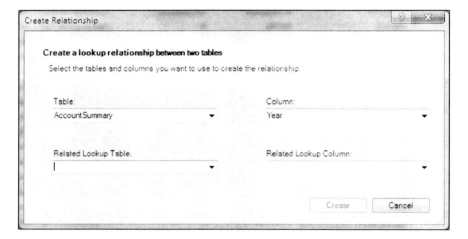

4. Leave **Table** set to **AccountSummary** and change **Column** to **Account Number**.
5. Use the drop-down in **Related Lookup Table** to select **Accounts Default**.
6. Use the drop-down in **Related Lookup Column** to select **Account Number** and click on **Create**.

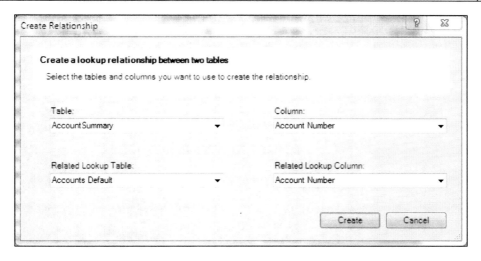

Now, we have a PowerPivot sheet that was pasted into our original PowerPivotSample file and a saved Excel 2013 file. Let's grab a SQL table to finish this off.

Connecting via SQL Server

For our example, we'll connect to the `Account Index Master` table named `GL00105` to get account segments. We could use DAX formulas to split out the segments, but then I wouldn't have this great example.

To connect SQL Server data to PowerPivot, follow these steps:

1. In the PowerPivot for Excel window, click on **Home | From Other Sources | Microsoft SQL Server**.

2. Use the drop-down next to **Server Name** to select the **SQL Server with GP** data.

3. Select your authentication method. I'm using **Windows Authentication**. If you have a specific SQL Server login, you can select **Use SQL Server Authentication** and enter a username and password.

 Because Dynamics GP 2013 encrypts the logins used for SQL Server, you cannot use your login and password for Dynamics GP here. If you are not using **Windows Authentication**, you must have a separate SQL password.

4. Set **Database name** to our sample database as **TWO** and click on **Next**.

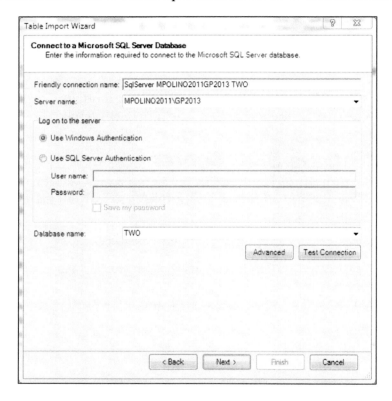

5. Mark the **Select from a list of tables and views to choose the data to import** checkbox and click on **Next**.

6. Scroll down and check the box next to **GL00105**, then click on **Finish**.

When scrolling, SQL Server tables are listed at the top and views are below them. If we were looking for the **Account Summary** view that we've used in previous chapters, we would need to scroll past all the tables alphabetically until the alphabet starts over with view names.

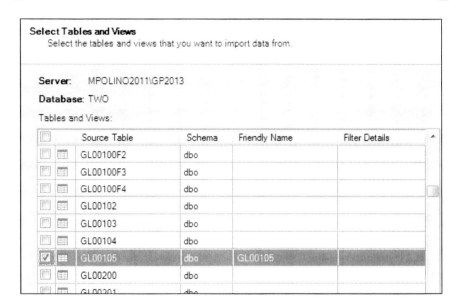

Select Tables and Views
Select the tables and views that you want to import data from.

Server: MPOLINO2011\GP2013

Database: TWO

Tables and Views:

		Source Table	Schema	Friendly Name	Filter Details	
☐	▦	GL00100F2	dbo			
☐	▦	GL00100F3	dbo			
☐	▦	GL00100F4	dbo			
☐	▦	GL00102	dbo			
☐	▦	GL00103	dbo			
☐	▦	GL00104	dbo			
☑	▦	GL00105	dbo	GL00105		
☐	▦	GL00200	dbo			
☐	▦	GL00201	dbo			

7. When the import finishes, click on **Close**.

ACTINDX ▼	ACTNUMBR_1 ▼	ACTNUMBR_2 ▼	ACTNUMBR_3 ▼	ACTNUMBR_4 ▼	ACTNUMBR_5 ▼	ACTNUMST ▼	DEX_ROW_ID ▼
1	000	1100	00			000-1100-00	1
2	000	1110	00			000-1110-00	2
3	000	1120	00			000-1120-00	3
4	000	1130	00			000-1130-00	4
5	000	1140	00			000-1140-00	5
6	000	1200	00			000-1200-00	6
7	000	1205	00			000-1205-00	7
8	000	1210	00			000-1210-00	8

An important PowerPivot performance point is to only bring in the columns and tables that you need. I learned this the hard way with a very small model that took more than a minute to refresh. After I cleaned out the columns, it refreshed in about 15 seconds. Apply this to very large models, and you can see huge performance gains.

Now let's connect this table as well. To connect **GL00105** to **AccountSummary**, follow these steps:

1. In the PowerPivot for Excel window, click on the **AccountSummary** tab.
2. Select **Design | Create Relationship**.
3. The **Create Relationship** box will open.
4. Leave **Table** set to **AccountSummary** and change **Column** to **Account Number**.
5. Use the drop-down in **Related Lookup Table** to select **GL00105**.
6. Use the drop-down in **Related Lookup Column** to select **ACTNUMST** and click on **Create**.

Learning about relationships

You'll notice that the only option is to connect a single field from one table to a single field from another table. In Dynamics GP, there are scenarios where more than one column is required to establish a relationship. For example, when connecting Sales Order Processing headers to detail records, both **Document ID** and **Document Type** are required. In that scenario, you'll need to create a combined key.

A combined key is simply a formula used to combine the values from multiple columns into one column. You'll need to combine the keys in each table and then join them based on the combined column. The same principle applies when using the VLookup formula in Microsoft Excel. You can only look up from one column to the other. If multiple columns are required, you have to combine them first. This shouldn't seem too foreign for longtime Excel users. Usually, building a combined key is simply a matter of adding the appropriate columns together into a single new column using a formula.

In many cases, PowerPivot will try to automatically join tables for you. With Dynamics GP tables, it will frequently get the joins wrong. This is because PowerPivot tries to match on fields with the same name across different tables. Dynamics GP uses `Dex_Row_ID` as a unique identifier within a table, but `Dex_Row_ID` doesn't correspond across tables. `Dex_Row_ID 1` in a table has no relationship to `Dex_Row_ID 1` in a different table, so it can't be used to join tables. Consequently, you'll need to check and adjust any automatic joins.

PowerPivot in Microsoft Excel offers an alternative way to create relationships. In your `PowerPivot Sample` file, select **Diagram View** from the **Home** tab. You'll see your current relationships diagramed out. This view can also be used to create relationships via drag and connect.

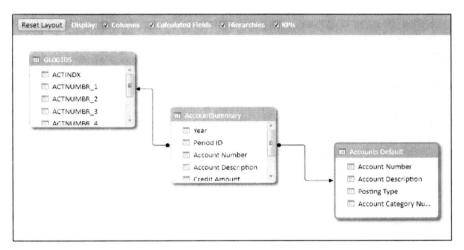

Creating a pivot table

We've looked at a bunch of tools to bring data into PowerPivot and link our data together. The payoff comes when you start to analyze this data with pivot tables. So, let's create a pivot table from PowerPivot data.

1. In the `PowerPivotSample.xlsx` file that we've been working with, select the **Home** tab.
2. Click the **PivotTable** icon in the center.

3. Select **New Worksheet** in the pop-up box.

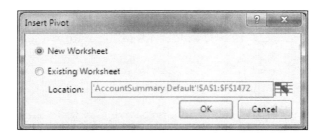

An empty pivot table opens in Excel 2013.

 Notice that, unlike a regular Excel pivot table, there are three sources of data for you to choose fields from.

4. Drag **Account Number** from under **AccountSummary** and drop it in the **Rows** area to analyze data by account.

5. Also under **AccountSummary**, drag **Year** into **Filters** to limit our data to specific years.

6. For the last item under **AccountSummary**, drag **CalculatedColumn1** into the **Values** section.

7. Under **Accounts Default**, drag **Posting Type** into **Filters**, under **Year**. This way we can easily analyze **Balance Sheet** versus **Income Statement** accounts.

8. Under **GL00105**, drag **ACTNUMBER_1** into the **Columns** area.

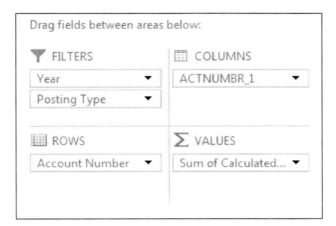

9. Change the **Year** filter at the top to **2017** and change the **Posting Type** filter to **Income Statement**.

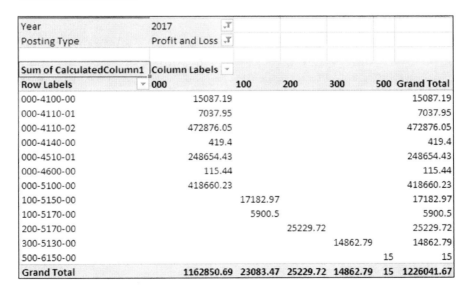

Year	2017					
Posting Type	Profit and Loss					
Sum of CalculatedColumn1	Column Labels					
Row Labels	000	100	200	300	500	Grand Total
000-4100-00	15087.19					15087.19
000-4110-01	7037.95					7037.95
000-4110-02	472876.05					472876.05
000-4140-00	419.4					419.4
000-4510-01	248654.43					248654.43
000-4600-00	115.44					115.44
000-5100-00	418660.23					418660.23
100-5150-00		17182.97				17182.97
100-5170-00		5900.5				5900.5
200-5170-00			25229.72			25229.72
300-5130-00				14862.79		14862.79
500-6150-00					15	15
Grand Total	1162850.69	23083.47	25229.72	14862.79	15	1226041.67

This pivot table shows off some of the advantages of PowerPivot over regular Excel 2013 pivot tables. Joining multiple tables in Excel would require significant data manipulation, or the source data would need to already be combined using a view or a tool such as the Analysis Cubes for Excel product from Microsoft.

Understanding the Excel data model

We've focused on using the PowerPivot window to connect multiple sources and built an Excel pivot table. Because of the power of DAX formulas and other PowerPivot specific features, I wanted you to get comfortable with how the PowerPivot Windows work. But with Excel 2013, Microsoft has quietly slipped some PowerPivot functionality into regular Excel features as well.

If you just want to join a couple of tables together, you don't have to explicitly use PowerPivot. You can use the new Excel Data Model. The Excel Data Model uses PowerPivot features behind the scenes. When you build pivot tables with the data model, the xVelocity engine is used automatically, you get the speed of PowerPivot, and you get great performance with a large number of rows. Plus, this works even if the PowerPivot add-on isn't explicitly activated. It's sort of a stealthy PowerPivot.

Let's look at how to join two tables and build a pivot table using the Excel Data Model. To do this, follow these steps:

1. In a new Excel 2013 worksheet, select the **Data** tab and click on **Existing Connections** from the ribbon.

2. Click on **Browse for More** and navigate to where you installed the GP 2013 Data Connections for the sample company. In my case, this was `c:\GP2013XL\Data Connections\TWO`.

3. Select the `Financial` directory and double-click on **TWO AccountSummary**.

4. Select **PivotTable Report**, check **Add this Data to the Data Model**, and click on **OK**.

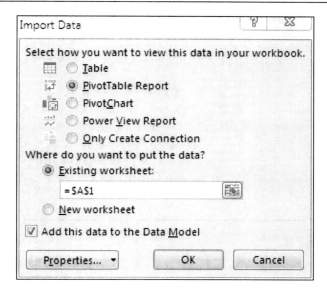

5. Click on cell E1 to select a location outside the pivot table area.

6. Select the **Data** tab and click on **Existing Connections** from the ribbon.

7. Click on **Browse for More** and navigate to where you installed the GP 2013 Data Connections for the sample company. In my case, this was `c:\GP2013XL\Data Connections\TWO`.

8. Select the `Financial` directory and double-click on **TWO Accounts**.

9. Select **Only Create Connection**, check **Add this Data to the Data Model**, and click on **OK**.

10. Click inside the pivot table area.

11. Under **PivotTable Fields,** select **All**.

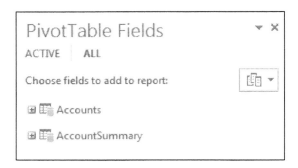

12. Now we have two tables to work with; let's start building a pivot table:

    ° Under **AccountSummary**, drag **Account Number to Rows**

    ° Under **AccountSummary**, drag **Period Balance to Values**

    ° Under **Accounts**, drag **Posting Type into Columns**

13. As soon as we add a field from the second source, **Accounts**, Excel notices and asks us to create relationships.

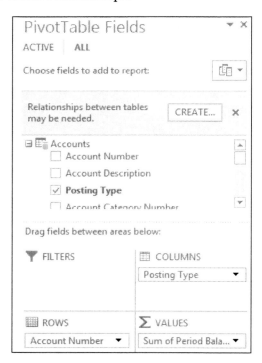

14. Click on **Create**.

15. Set the relationships using the drop-downs in each field. Set:
    ° **Table** to **Account Summary**
    ° **Column (Foreign)** to **Account Number**
    ° **Related Table** to **Accounts**
    ° **Related Column (Primary)** to **Account Number**

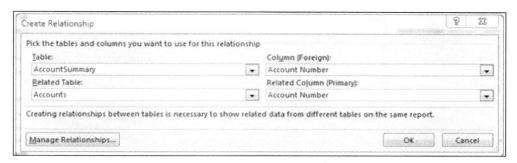

16. Click on **OK** to complete the relationship.

Now we have a pivot table with two related sources, and we never clicked on the **PowerPivot** tab. Click on **PowerPivot | Manage** to see what's going on behind the scenes.

Once the PowerPivot window opens, you'll see that PowerPivot is actually managing **Accounts**, **AccountSummary**, and the relationship. When using the Excel Data Model, the fact that it's being managed by PowerPivot is merely invisible to the end user.

Other source options

We've shown that PowerPivot provides the ability to easily combine and analyze data from different sources. For example, if you have a third-party accounts receivable application that integrates into Dynamics GP, you can still analyze that detailed data against the information in Dynamics GP. PowerPivot supports all the usual suspects: Excel, Text, SQL Server, Oracle, ODBC connections, and so on. But it also supports a couple of unusual connections, specifically Atom feeds, Reporting Services Reports, and the Windows Azure Marketplace.

About Atom feeds

Atom feeds are best known for syndicating blog content. The Atom format is an alternative to the more widely used RSS format. However, Atom feeds can be used for other things. Microsoft refers to these as OData feeds in PowerPivot. OData is a format based on Atom, and for our purposes, they are used interchangeably.

Atom feeds, with data designed to be consumed by tools such as PowerPivot, are still pretty rare, but imagine the opportunity to bring in currency data, stock market data, public financial data from competitors, or even pricing data from Amazon to analyze competitive pricing against data in Dynamics GP.

We'll do a quick example just to show you how this works. Netflix offers an experimental OData feed into their movie database. We'll bring in movies released after 2011 as a quick example. To bring in this Atom feed, follow these steps:

1. Open a new Excel 2013 workbook and select **PowerPivot | Manage**.

2. Click on **From Data Service | From OData Feed**.

3. In the **Data Feed Url** box, enter

    ```
    http://odata.netflix.com/Catalog/Titles?$filter=ReleaseYear gt
    2011.
    ```

4. Click on **Advanced**.

5. Set **Max Received Message** size to 999999999999999 (the number 9 keyed 15 times). This will prevent this feed with a large amount of data from failing.

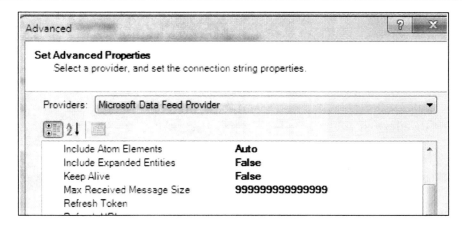

6. Click **OK | Next | Finish**.

7. When the process finishes showing success, click on **Close**.

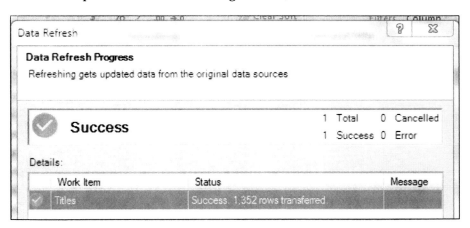

We now have Netflix movies released after 2011, and the data is easily updated by clicking on the **Refresh** button in PowerPivot.

I'm hopeful that as more people move to Excel 2013 and PowerPivot, we'll see more feeds designed for analysis of data, but even if we don't, this is still useful to organizations. Both SharePoint and SQL Server Reporting Services can generate Atom feeds, making this an easy way to share and consume information from other parts of the business.

SQL Server Reporting Services (SSRS)

In more secure environments, it's not unusual for users to only get information only via reports and have no access to the underlying SQL data. SQL Server Reporting Services, known as SSSRS or SSRS, is often the vehicle for delivering those reports.

If you only have access to SSRS, that doesn't mean that you're out of luck. Starting with SQL Reporting Services 2008 R2, there are a number of options for getting data out of SSRS. We looked at exporting to Excel from SSRS in *Chapter 1, Getting Data from Dynamics GP 2013 to Excel 2013*, but SSRS can also generate Atom feeds, and PowerPivot can natively connect to SSRS reports.

Generating an Atom feed from an SSRS report

To generate an Atom feed from an SSRS report:

1. Run an SSRS report. Any of the default GP SSRS reports work fine for this.

2. Click on the orange feed icon next to the printer icon on the toolbar.

3. Save the file when prompted.

Now you have an Atom feed that can be selected in PowerPivot's **Data Feed Url** field like we did in the last example.

For reports that are summarized, the Atom feed actually returns the underlying data. This means that the **Account Summary Trial Balance** report actually returns the underlying data for each period, not just one line per account.

SSRS native connections

Another option for SSRS reports is to connect to them directly via PowerPivot. Unfortunately, there appears to be a bug when connecting to the prebuilt GP SSRS reports. PowerPivot connects and can preview the data but returns the error, XML `parsing...Illegal xml character` when you click on **Finish**. This is likely a design flaw in the prebuilt GP SSRS reports. Since many companies have built their own SSRS reports connected to GP data, we'll still look at how this works. To import from SSRS into PowerPivot:

1. Open a new Excel 2013 worksheet and select **PowerPivot | Manage**.
2. Click **From Other Sources | Report**.
3. Click on **Browse**, and in the **Name** box, enter:
   - The location of the report server
   - The path to the report
   - The report name

4. All of this should be on one line. For example, the location could be `http://mpolino2011/ReportServer/GP2013beta2/TWO/Financial/ Trial Balance Summary`.

   In our example, `http://mpolino2011/ReportServer` is the report server location, `Trial Balance Summary` is the report name, and everything in the middle is the path to the report.

5. Click on **Open**. The report opens in the view window, and you can interact with the report to set parameters such as dates or accounts.
6. Set the parameters to the report.
7. Click on **View Report** to run the report.
8. Click on **Next | Finish** to bring the data into PowerPivot.

Windows Azure Marketplace

With Excel 2013, Microsoft is offering additional data options via the Windows Azure Marketplace. The Marketplace is like an app store for data. There is actually a mix of free and paid data sources and applications for use with PowerPivot and Excel 2013.

A couple of the early items that caught my eye were Dun & Bradstreet company credit information, CCH sales tax rates, and currency rates. I could certainly see the benefit of being able to mash up my customer, sales, and collection information from Dynamics GP against D&B credit ratings. I bet that I would find some interesting relationships.

Since D&B requires a paid subscription, we won't use that as an example. We'll do a quick example with some free data. To pull in a feed from the Windows Azure Marketplace, follow these steps:

1. Open Excel 2013 and select **PowerPivot | Manage**.

2. Select **From Data Service | From Windows Azure Marketplace**.

3. On the left-hand side, under **Type**, click on **Data**.

4. On the left-hand side, under **Price**, click on **Free**.

5. Find `Barcelona Car Registrations for 2009` and click on **Subscribe**.

6. Sign in using a Microsoft account (formerly Windows Live ID).

7. Scroll to the end of the data and click on **Select Query**.

8. Click on **Next** | **Finish**.

9. After the import succeeds, click on **Close** to transfer the data into PowerPivot.

Now we have Barcelona car registration data in PowerPivot to connect or compare against our data from Dynamics GP 2013. Again, this could be currency rates, sales tax rates, credit data, or just about anything else that's available in the Windows Azure Marketplace. The option to access paid data opens up whole new possibilities for analysis.

The Windows Azure Marketplace is really using an OData feed behind the scenes to transfer information from these data providers into PowerPivot.

More PowerPivot options

PowerPivot is huge. You could write whole books about it. In fact, people have written whole books about it. I've focused on getting data into PowerPivot, because this is the area that is going to be the least familiar to Dynamics GP users. Once the data comes into an Excel pivot table, the processes of pivoting data, reporting off of data, and building dashboards is essentially the same regardless of how the data comes in. Given our limited time and space, I did want to highlight a few things that we won't spend much time on.

Millions of rows of data

PowerPivot allows you to work with millions of rows of data. The sample data in GP 2013 doesn't even come close to this level, but don't lose sight of how powerful this can be. I had someone come up to me with a million rows in their Analytical Accounting tables, and that data was growing by tens of thousands per month. I have other companies that I work with that have 10 years of GL history and their GL numbers are well over 5 million. With at least one debit and credit per transaction, it's easy to build a pivot table that will overwhelm Excel 2013.

If you would like to play with some high-volume data, Microsoft offers sample sets at `http://www.microsoft.com/en-us/download/details. aspx?displaylang=en&id=102`.

DAX formulas

We haven't done much with DAX formulas, but they are incredibly powerful, more powerful than Excel formulas in many cases. DAX formulas support filtering, additional time calculations, summarizing data, and much, much more. The single best resource for understanding DAX formulas that I've found is Rob Collie's book *DAX Formulas for PowerPivot*. You can get more information at `http://www. powerpivotpro.com/the-book/`.

SharePoint

PowerPivot is now part of Excel 2013, but it's also part of SharePoint. There is a feature of SharePoint that allows you to deploy a PowerPivot-based Excel workbook to a company SharePoint site. Users are able to interact with the sheets and refresh them.

 Using SharePoint is the only way to automatically refresh PowerPivot data without clicking on the **Refresh** button.

If your organization doesn't run SharePoint or doesn't want the hassle of deploying and managing PowerPivot-based Excel sheets, Pivotstream offers a hosting and sharing option that is inexpensive, robust and secure. You can find out more at www.pivotstream.com.

Resources

We can't cover everything in this book, but there are some great resources available around PowerPivot. A couple of my favorites are:

- **PowerPivotPro** (www.powerpivotpro): PowerPivotPro is a great site, full of creative tips for getting the most out of PowerPivot. It's run by SQL Server MVP and one of the founding engineers of PowerPivot during his time at Microsoft, Rob Collie.

- **Mr. Excel** (www.mrexcel.com): Bill Jelen (Mr. Excel) is a Microsoft MVP for Excel, an author and a huge of fan of PowerPivot for data analysis. His site contains a ton of resources for getting the most out of Excel and PowerPivot.

The addition of PowerPivot to Microsoft Excel 2013 lets you take Dynamics GP 2013 information and analyze it in ways that would have been much harder without this tool. Processes that could have taken months of meetings with database administrators to get and aggregate information can now be done in minutes. This opens the power of dashboards to incorporate information from even more sources, both from inside and outside the organization.

Summary

We've just scratched the surface of what can be done with PowerPivot. In truth, many of you will eventually move to PowerPivot as the primary source for Excel-based dashboards. PowerPivot is the future, but the idea of PowerPivot is intimidating to many people, so we've built our dashboards first using basic Excel functionality. Since dashboards often evolve as they mature, changing the source to PowerPivot becomes a logical move during one of the dashboard iterations. Users won't see much difference, except that they may have improved their performance. Builders get a huge advantage in both performance and flexibility.

This chapter on PowerPivot, and the next chapter on slightly crazy stuff, are designed to help you extend the solution that was built in the first eight chapters. They both stand on their own, and they complement the work that you've already done. *Chapter 10, Slightly Crazy Stuff* contains a number of items that are important for dashboard building but didn't quite fit anywhere else.

10
Slightly Crazy Stuff

For this last chapter, I have a few things that didn't quite fit into our dashboard. Some of them are a little advanced, and others would add more complexity to our basic dashboard than I wanted. We'll wrap up the book with a look at:

- Built-in ratios
- Current Ratio
- Microsoft Dashboard
- Negative data bars
- Quick Analysis

Using built-in ratios

One of the things that can be hard to do when building your own dashboard is to calculate ratios. Fortunately, you're in luck. Microsoft Dynamics GP 2013 provides a set of built-in ratios including:

- Quick Ratio
- Debt to Equity Ratio
- Gross Profit Margin
- AR Days Outstanding
- Receivables Turnover

 To use these stored procedures, users will need Execute rights to the procedure in SQL server.

These ratios are great, but they are harder to use because they are based on stored procedures. Let's take a quick look at, well, the quick ratio. To get the quick ratio for the two sample company, follow these steps:

1. Create a new sheet in Microsoft Excel 2013.

2. In cell B2, type 12/31/17, and in cell C2, type Year. We will need to use these for the UserDate and TimeUnit parameters in the stored procedure.

3. Put the cursor in cell b4.

4. Select **Data | From Other Sources | From Microsoft Query**.

5. Select the Dynamics GP data source. By default, this data source is named DynGP.

6. Scroll down and click the plus sign (**+**) to expand **GL00100**.

7. Pick **ACTINDX** and hit the right arrow.

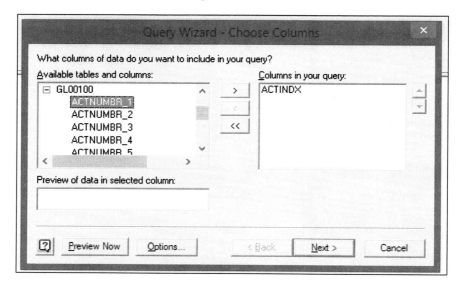

8. Click **Next** three times, then click on **Finish**. This is really just a placeholder until we put in our own SQL for the stored procedure. We can't directly enter a stored procedure, so we have to do this workaround. It really doesn't matter what table and fields we select; we're going to override them.

9. On the **Import Data** box, select **Properties**.

10. Click on **Definition**.

11. Set **Command Type** to SQL.

12. In the white **Command Text** box at the bottom, type `exec seeGLQuickRatioKPI @UserDate=?, @TimeUnit=?`.

13. Click on **OK** twice to finish.

14. The **Enter Parameter Value** box will open for **Parameter 1**. Select cell B2 (value 12/31/17) as parameter 1.

15. Check the boxes for **Use this value/reference for future refreshes** and **Refresh automatically when cell value changes** and click on **OK**.

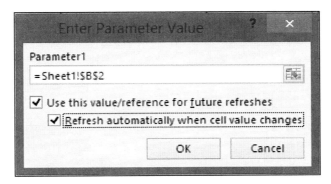

16. The **Enter Parameter Value** box will open for **Parameter 2**. Select cell C2 (value Year) as Parameter 2.

17. Check the boxes for **Use this value/reference for future refreshes** and **Refresh automatically when cell value changes** and click **OK**.

12/31/2017	Year			
CurrentQuickRatio	PreviousQuickRatio	LastYearQuickRatio	CurrPrevPercChange	CurrLYPercChange
0.44	-0.16	375.00%	0.00%	

18. With that, quick ratio data appears for use in your dashboard.

> **Year** or **Period** are options for the time unit parameter in these stored procedures.

The stored procedures for the pre-built ratios are:

Ratio	Command to run stored procedure
Quick ratio	`exec seeGLQuickRatioKPI @UserDate=?, @TimeUnit=?`
Debt to equity ratio	`exec seeGLDebtToEquityKPI @UserDate=?, @TimeUnit=?`
Gross profit margin	`exec seeGLGrossProfitMarginKPI @UserDate=?, @TimeUnit=?`
AR days outstanding	`exec seeARDaysOutstandingKPI @UserDate=?, @TimeUnit=?`
Receivables turnover	`exec seeGLReceivablesTurnoverKPI @UserDate=?,@TimeUnit=?`

Current Ratio

One of the things you'll notice from this list is that the current ratio is missing. Jared Hall of Microsoft was kind enough to share the code to create the current ratio. This code is provided as is, so if you have issues, don't call Jared! Once you've created the stored procedure, you can run it just like the others. The code to run it is:

```
exec seeGLCurrentRatioKPI @UserDate=?, @TimeUnit=?
```

I've made the code for this stored procedure available for download at `https://www.box.com/s/szt1oej6op7pet3r1wzj` (short link: `http://bit.ly/Z1r9Bu`). It's also available from Packt Publishing as part of the code download for this book. Simply run the code in SQL Server Enterprise Manager for each company database. Then, you'll be able to run the Current Ratio stored procedure.

Microsoft Dashboard

As I was working on this book, Microsoft found the dashboard religion for Dynamics GP. It released a sample dashboard for users to play with. You can get the sample dashboard at `http://blogs.msdn.com/b/gp/archive/2012/11/06/business-intelligence-investigation.aspx`.

Microsoft's sample dashboard has too many rows and columns for my taste. It looks too much like a report on the left-hand side. We know that executives don't want to see reports. Still, it's a good start, and it's something for you to play with.

Negative data bars

We looked at data bars when we spent some time with Conditional Formatting.
In Microsoft Excel 2013, we can have negative data bars as well as positive data
bars. We also get different color formatting for the negatives. To illustrate this,
follow these steps:

1. Open a blank Excel 2013 workbook.

2. In cells B3 through B6, type `January`, `February`, `March`, `April`.

3. In cells C3 through C6, type `100`, `200`, `10`, `-50`.

4. Highlight cells C3 through C6.

5. Select **Conditional Formatting | Data Bars**. Pick the first option on the left-hand side under **Gradient Fill**.

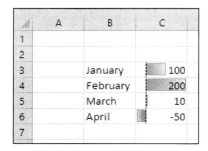

Positive items are displayed in blue and negatives are in red.

Quick Analysis

There is another tool that is new inside of Microsoft Excel 2013. It's known as Quick Analysis. Quick Analysis is a great tool for giving users different looks at data without having to commit to something like creating a chart.

Let's use the data we created for negative data bars to look at Quick Analysis. To do that, follow these steps:

1. Select cell C5.

2. Right-click and select **Quick Analysis**.

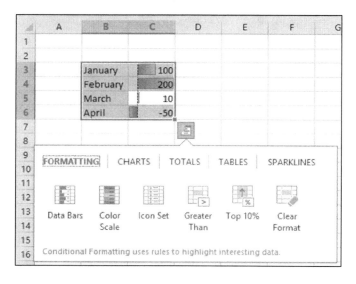

3. A set of options pop up. Pick **Charts** and hover over **Clustered Column** to preview a column chart. Clicking **Clustered Column** will actually create a chart.

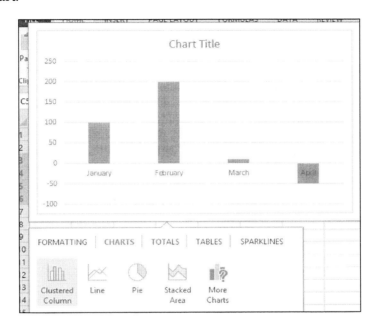

4. Select **Totals** and hover over **Sum**, then **Average**, then the other options to see the different values.

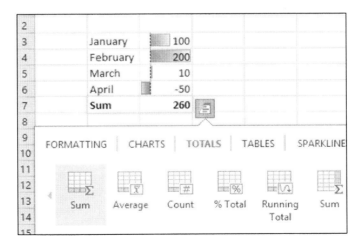

Clicking on any of the options activates that option in the sheet.

Summary

This chapter is like a goody bag. There are a number of things in here that can really make a dashboard sing. Each dashboard is unique. Companies have many of the same information needs, but often they need to be presented in different ways. Tools like the ones in this chapter give you options to customize a dashboard for your organization.

We've built a dashboard for Microsoft Dynamics GP 2013 from scratch using Microsoft Excel 2013. Along the way, we've explored a number of different ways to put the pieces together so that you can build one for your organization. A basic, Excel-based dashboard simply uses all of the tools common to Excel pros: pivot tables, charts, slicers, and formatting to present data in a way that's easy to understand. Connecting Excel data to the source data in Dynamics GP 2013 makes that data easy to refresh as well. Now it's your turn. Go experiment. Build something. Fail. Build something else. Succeed a little. Finally, build something great.

Index

A

Account Description field 150
Account Index for Drillback 167
Account Index for Journal 167
AccountSummary Default report 68
ACE 30, 31
Add Filter button 44
Analysis Cubes for Excel. *See* ACE
AR days outstanding 238
Atom feed
    about 226-228
    generating, from SSRS report 228
auto refresh
    versus manual refresh 46, 47

B

backgrounds
    color, adding 191
    creating 190, 191
    Fill Color feature 191
    inserting 193-195
    picture, inserting 192, 193
bar chart
    about 115
    building, steps for 115, 116
    with trend line 129
BI 32
BI360
    URL 33
BIO
    URL 33
BizNet
    URL 33

built-in ratios
    about 235-237
    stored procedures 238
Business Intelligence. *See* BI

C

CAL 34
calculations, Excel Report Builder 57
cash pivot table
    creating 72-74
Cash tab
    unhiding 188
chart
    about 113
    formatting 128
    selecting 113
    trend line, adding 130
Citrix
    drill down, with Excel 2013 178
    drill down, with GP 2013 178
cleaning up
    dashboard 182-188
    final clean up 200, 201
Client Access License. *See* CAL
color, background
    adding 191
color scales
    about 104
    adjusting, steps for 105, 106
    setting up 104
Command text box 52
Command Text window 77
Comments option 28

Corporate Performance Management.
See **CPM**
CPM 32
Create Sparklines box 134
current ratio
  about 238
  URL 238

D

dashboard
  about 7, 87
  cleaning up 182-188
  displaying 86
  final cleanup items 200, 201
  holding, sheet creating for 87
  Receivables, linking 186, 187
  Sales by City, linking 186, 187
  screenshot 115, 140, 162, 196, 197
data
  copying, into PowerPivot 208, 209
  getting, to Excel 64, 65
  pasting, into PowerPivot 208, 209
  refreshing 202
Data Analysis Expression Language (DAX)
  about 206
data bars
  about 99-101, 104
  adding, steps for 102, 103
  URL 104
database-level security
  about 39, 40
  access, granting to reporting roles 41
  user, addding to SQL server 40
data mart 33
data warehouse 30, 33
DAX formulas 232
debt data
  URL 196
debt to equity ratio 238
deFacto Performance Management
  URL 33
Dex.ini file 9
Disable resizing and moving checkbox,
  slicer 148
Display totals at the end of each list 58

Document Date timeline slicer 155
Don't move or size with cells option 147
doughnut, speedometer chart
  building 122
  cutting, in half 123, 124
drill down
  Account Index for Drillback 167
  Account Index for Journal 167
  background 165, 166
  complex 178
  complex scenarios, offering 179, 180
  journal entry drill down issues, fixing 170
  link, structure 171-176
  to GP 2013 on Citrix, with Excel 2013
    installed 178
  using 166, 167
  using, in Microsoft Dynamics GP 2013 165
  with Excel 2013, on Citrix 178
  with Excel 2013, on Terminal Server 178
  with GP 2013, on Citrix 178
  with GP 2013, on Terminal Server 178
Drill Down Builder 177
drill down elements
  Act=OPEN 171
  Cmp=TWO 171
  Db=GP2013 171
  dgpp://DGPB/? 171
  Func=OpenJournalInq 171
  JRNENTRY=27 171
  Prod=0 171
  RCTRXSEQ=1 172
  Srv=MPOLINO2011 171
  TRXDATE=01/01/2014 172
DynamicAccounting.net table resource
  URL 24
Dynamics GP 2013. *See* **Microsoft**
  Dynamics GP 2013

E

e-mail option 203
Excel
  Navigation List export to 14
  pivot tables 63
  SmartList, exporting from 8, 9
Excel 2013
  Excel reports, running from 45

formula-based link, building 167-169
security 42, 43
Excel-based Business Intelligence
  options 33
Excel-Based Corporate Performance
  Management options 33
Excel-based dashboard, sharing options
  about 202
  e-mail option 203
  network sharing 203
  options 202
  SharePoint, downloading via 204
  SharePoint Excel Services, hosting via 204
  SkyDrive, downloading via 204
  SkyDrive, hosting via 203
Excel data
  reformatting 47, 49
Excel data model
  about 222
  used, for building pivot table 222-225
  used, for joining two tables 222-225
Excel file
  combining, with PowerPivot 211-213
Excel macros
  creating 10, 11
Excel Report Builder
  about 54
  calculations with 57
  options button 58, 59
  publish report window 59, 60
  report, building with 55, 56
  restrictions 57
Excel Report Builder pivot tables
  about 78, 79
  running, steps for 80
  using 80
Excel reports
  about 35
  and security, URL 43
  modifying 47
  publishing, requisites 60
  refreshable 35
  running 43
  security 35
Excel reports, modifying
  about 47
  Excel data, reformatting 47-49

source data, modifying 49-52
Excel reports, running
  from Dynamics GP 2013 43-45
  from Excel 2013 45
  manual versus auto refresh 46, 47
Excel sheet
  adding from current workbook 210
exponential 133
Export range option 28
Export Solutions option 13

F

F9
  URL 33
Fill Color feature 191
Flash Fill feature 47, 49
Format Data Labels section 119
Format Data Options sidebar 123
Format Data Point sidebar 123, 124
formatting
  about 92-94, 108-111
  recommendations 110, 111
Format Trendline sidebar 132
formula-based link
  building, in Excel 2013 167-169

G

Get Pivot Data
  about 87
  formatting 92-94
  net income pivot table 91, 92
  revenue pivot table 88, 89
GP 2013 data connections
  pivot tables, creating from 67, 68
GP 2013 Excel report data
  pivot tables, creating from 64
green/yellow/red limit 107, 108
Gross profit margin 238

H

Header element, timeline 157
headers
  about 182
  adding 182

hide items with no data option 149
hyperlinks 162, 163, 164

I

icon sets
  about 95
  setting up 95-99
Import Data window 75, 77
income pivot table
  building 71, 72
Insert tab 116

J

Jet Reports
  URL 33
Journal article
  URL 206
journal entry drill down
  issues, fixing 170

L

licensing model 34
line
  adding, steps for 117
linear 132
links, drill back
  making invisible 185
links, drill down
  for journal entry 171
  structure 171-176
logarithmic 132
logo
  adding 189
  adding, steps for 189, 190

M

Management Reporter
  about 26
  Comments option 28
  Export range option 28
  Microsoft Excel options section 28
  Report Type option 28

manual refresh
  versus auto refresh 46, 47
Microsoft Dashboard
  about 238
  sample dashboard, URL 238
Microsoft Dynamics GP 2013
  about 7
  Analysis Cubes for Excel (ACE) 30, 31
  built-in ratios 235
  drill downs, using 165
  Excel reports, running from 43-45
  licensing model 34
  Management Reporter 26, 28
  Microsoft Query 17
  report writer 15, 16
  SQL Server Management Studio 28, 29
  SQL Server Reporting Services (SSRS)
    report 24- 26
  third-party solutions 32-34
Microsoft Excel 2013
  negative data bars 239
  quick analysis 240
Microsoft Excel options section 28
Microsoft Query
  about 17
  direct connection, adding between
    GP and Excel 17-24
Move and size with cells option 147
Move but don't size with cells option 147
moving average 133
Mr. Excel
  URL 233
Ms Query. See Microsoft Query
multicompany report 58

N

Navigation List export
  about 13
  to Excel 14
needle, speedometer chart
  building 124-127
negative data bars 239, 240
Net Income graph 144
net income pivot table 91, 92
network share security 36-38
network sharing option 203

O

ODBC 17
ODC
  about 53
  connection file, applying to specific
      workbook 53, 54
  connection information, saving 53
Office Clip Art search box 189
Office Data Connection. *See* ODC
Office Data Connection (ODC) file 203
OLAP Office
  URL 33
OLAP tool 30
Online Analytical Processing.
      See OLAP tool
Open Database Connectivity. *See* ODBC
options button, Excel Report Builder
  about 58
  Display totals at the end of each list 58
  multicompany report 58

P

Perceptual Edge
  URL 133
Period ID slicer 144
period slicer 143
picture, background
  inserting 192, 193
pie chart
  about 118
  building, steps for 118-121
PivotTable Fields box 66
pivot tables
  about 63
  building, steps for 65, 66
  cash pivot table, creating 72-74
  connected pivot tables, creating from
      inside Excel 74
  copying 71
  creating, from GP 2013 data
      connections 67, 68
  creating, from GP 2013 Excel report data 64
  creating, from PowerPivot data 219-222
  data, getting to Excel 64, 65
  Excel report based on 80

Excel Report Builder pivot tables 78, 79
  income pivot table, building 71, 72
  receivables pivot table, adding 77, 78
  revenue pivot table, building 68-70
  sales pivot table, building 74-76
  two tables building, Excel data model
      used 222-225
Plaza One 104
polynomial 132
POSITION AND LAYOUT section,
      slicer 148
Posting Type filter 72
power 132
PowerPivot
  about 205, 232
  basics 207
  data, copying into 208, 209
  data, pasting into 208, 209
  data rows 232
  DAX formulas 232
  Excel file, combining 211-213
  Excel file getting, steps for 211
  Excel sheet, adding from current
      workbook 210, 211
  relationship between two datasets,
      creating 214, 215
  resources 233
  SharePoint 233
  SQL Server, connecting via 215-218
PowerPivot data
  pivot table, creating from 219-222
PowerPivotPro
  URL 233
Power View reports
  about 81
  building, steps for 81-84
properties section, slicer 147
Prophix
  URL 33
publish report window, Excel Report
      Builder 59, 60

Q

Qbica
  URL 33
quick analysis

about 240
data 240, 241
quick ratio 238

R

Receivables
linking, to dashboard 186, 187
receivables pivot table
adding 77, 78
receivables turnover 238
Refresh button 227
regression analysis 129
relationships 218, 219
release to manufacturing (RTM) 170
reporting roles
access, granting to 41
Reports Options 156
Report Type option 28
report writer, Microsoft Dynamics GP 2013
about 15
data, getting in Escel 15, 16
resources, PowerPivot
about 233
Mr. Excel 233
PowerPivotPro 233
restrictions, Excel Report Builder 57
revenue pivot table
about 88
building 68-70
Revenue tab 88
Revenue worksheet 141
rpt_accounting manager role 40

S

Sales by City
linking, to dashboard 186, 187
sales pivot table
building 74-76
Scrollbar element, timeline 158
Section Label element, timeline 157
security, Excel reports
database-level security 36-40
Excel 2013 security 36, 42
Excel security message, disabling 42, 43
network share security 36-38

SharePoint
about 233
downloading via 204
SharePoint Excel Services
sharing via 204
show items with no data last option 149
SkyDrive
downloading via 204
hosting via 203
slicers
about 141, 150
additional options 148
connecting 144-146
creating, steps for 141-143
Don't move or size with cells option 147
hide items with no data option 149
Move but don't size with cells option 147
options 147
orientation 146
period slicer, adding 143, 144
show items with no data last option 149
visually indicate items with no data option
149
Year (Horizontal) slicer 149
Slicer Tools Options tab 146
SmartList
exporting from, to Excel 8, 9
SmartList builder manual
URL 61
SmartList Export Solutions
about 9
creating 11-13
Excel macros, creating 10, 11
Navigation List export 13
setting up 9, 10
Sort option 76
source data
modifying 49-52
sparklines
about 113, 134
adding 134-137
data, changing 137
deleting 137
idiosyncrasies 137
preparing for 134

Sparkline Tools Design tab 137
speedometer chart
  about 121
  doughnut, building 122
  doughnut, cutting in half 123, 124
  needle, building 124-127
  URL 129
SQL Server
  connecting, to PowerPivot 215-217
  user, adding to 40
SQL Server Management Studio
  about 28, 29
SQL Server Reporting Services. *See* SSRS
SSRS
  about 24-26, 228
  native connections 229
SSRS report
  Atom feed, generating from 228
stereotype 85
stored procedures, built-in ratios
  AR days outstanding 238
  debt to equity ratio 238
  Gross profit margin 238
  quick ratio 238
  receivables turnover 238
styles section, timeline 157
Support Debugging Tool
  URL 24

T

tables
  building, Excel data model
    used 222-225
Terminal Server
  drill down, with Excel 2013 178
  drill down, with GP 2013 178
third-party solutions 32
Time Level element, timeline 158
timeline
  about 151
  adding, for Top 10 Customers
    pivot table 151, 152
  Document Date timeline slicer 155
  Header element 157
  options 155
  Reports Options 156

Scrollbar element 158
Section Label element 157
styles section 157
Time Level element 158
Timeline Caption field 156
Timeline Tools Options ribbon 155
Timeline Caption field 156
Timeline Tools Options ribbon 155
Top 10 Customers pivot table
  about 151
  timeline, adding for 151, 152
  working 152-154
trend line
  adding, steps for 131, 132
  building, into chart 130
Two Account SummaryDefault
    Excel report 64
TWO AccountSummary Default item 44

U

user
  adding, to SQL server 40

V

visually indicate items with no
    data option 149
Vivid Reports
  URL 33

W

Windows Azure Marketplace 229-231

Y

Year (Horizontal) slicer 147-149

Thank you for buying
Building Dashboards with Microsoft Dynamics GP 2013 and Excel 2013

About Packt Publishing

Packt, pronounced 'packed', published its first book "Mastering phpMyAdmin for Effective MySQL Management" in April 2004 and subsequently continued to specialize in publishing highly focused books on specific technologies and solutions.

Our books and publications share the experiences of your fellow IT professionals in adapting and customizing today's systems, applications, and frameworks. Our solution based books give you the knowledge and power to customize the software and technologies you're using to get the job done. Packt books are more specific and less general than the IT books you have seen in the past. Our unique business model allows us to bring you more focused information, giving you more of what you need to know, and less of what you don't.

Packt is a modern, yet unique publishing company, which focuses on producing quality, cutting-edge books for communities of developers, administrators, and newbies alike. For more information, please visit our website: www.packtpub.com.

About Packt Enterprise

In 2010, Packt launched two new brands, Packt Enterprise and Packt Open Source, in order to continue its focus on specialization. This book is part of the Packt Enterprise brand, home to books published on enterprise software – software created by major vendors, including (but not limited to) IBM, Microsoft and Oracle, often for use in other corporations. Its titles will offer information relevant to a range of users of this software, including administrators, developers, architects, and end users.

Writing for Packt

We welcome all inquiries from people who are interested in authoring. Book proposals should be sent to author@packtpub.com. If your book idea is still at an early stage and you would like to discuss it first before writing a formal book proposal, contact us; one of our commissioning editors will get in touch with you.

We're not just looking for published authors; if you have strong technical skills but no writing experience, our experienced editors can help you develop a writing career, or simply get some additional reward for your expertise.

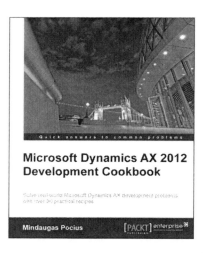

Microsoft Dynamics AX 2012 Development Cookbook

ISBN: 978-1-849684-64-4 Paperback: 372 pages

Solve real-world Microsoft Dynamics AX development problems with over 80 practical recipes

1. Develop powerful, successful Dynamics AX projects with efficient X++ code with this book and eBook

2. Proven recipes that can be reused in numerous successful Dynamics AX projects

3. Covers general ledger, accounts payable, accounts receivable, project modules and general functionality of Dynamics AX

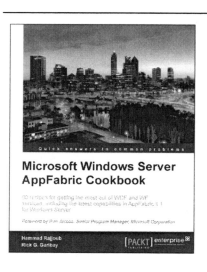

Microsoft Windows Server AppFabric Cookbook

ISBN: 978-1-849684-18-7 Paperback: 428 pages

60 recipes for getting the most out of WCF and WF services, including the latest capabilities in AppFabric 1.1 for Windows Server

1. Gain a solid understanding of the capabilities provided by Windows Server AppFabric with a pragmatic, hands-on, results-oriented approach with this book and eBook

2. Learn how to apply the WCF and WF skills you already have to make the most of what Windows Server AppFabric has to offer

3. Includes step-by-step recipes for developing highly scalable composite services that utilize the capabilities provided by Windows Server AppFabric including caching, hosting, monitoring and persistence.

Please check **www.PacktPub.com** for information on our titles

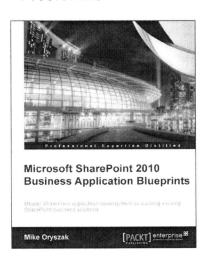

Microsoft SharePoint 2010 Business Application Blueprints

ISBN: 978-1-849683-60-9   Paperback: 282 pages

Master SharePoint application development by building exciting SharePoint business solutions

1. Instant SharePoint – Build nine exciting SharePoint business solutions

2. Expand your knowledge of the SharePoint platform so that you can tailor the sample solutions to your requirements

3. Learn how the different development techniques can be used in various situations to support both client side and server side development to solve different problems in different environments

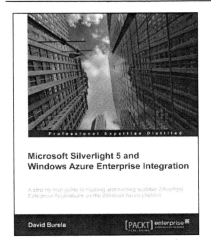

Microsoft Silverlight 5 and Windows Azure Enterprise Integration

ISBN: 978-1-849683-12-8   Paperback: 304 pages

A step-by-step guide to creating and running scalable Silverlight Enterprise Applications on the Windows Azure platform

1. This book and e-book details how enterprise Silverlight applications can be written to take advantage of the key features of Windows Azure to create scalable applications

2. Provides an overview of the Windows Azure platform and how the different technologies can be integrated within your enterprise application

3. Examines ways that distributed asynchronous systems can be created to allow scalable processing

Please check **www.PacktPub.com** for information on our titles

CPSIA information can be obtained at www.ICGtesting.com
Printed in the USA
LVOW05s0512131113

361108LV00018B/362/P

9 781849 689069